BED & BREAKFAST
and
UNIQUE INNS
of

Virginia

THIRD EDITION

A Pictorial Guide

Photography by Bruce W. Muncy
Text by Lynn Matthews Davis

Foreword by James "Bud" Robertson, Jr.

CRYSTAL SPRING PUBLISHING

BED & BREAKFAST AND UNIQUE INNS OF
VIRGINIA is published by Crystal Spring Publishing,
PO Box 8846, Roanoke, VA 24014.

Third Edition First Printed 1996

97 96 95 3 2 1

Printed in Hong Kong

Library of Congress ISSN 1087-5514

ISBN 0-9620996-7-8 Soft Cover

Other books by Crystal Spring Publishing:
BED & BREAKFAST AND UNIQUE INNS OF
VIRGINIA, First and Second Edition
BED & BREAKFAST AND UNIQUE INNS OF
PENNSYLVANIA

COVER PHOTOGRAPHS

front: The Inn at Meander Plantation

back: Caledonia Farm 1812

DEDICATED

By Lynn to my husband, Larry,
in committed love forever to
the most important person
of my life after honoring
the Lord.

By Bruce to Susan,
for the value of your friendship,
gift of your knowledge,
and joy of your love.

ACKNOWLEDGMENTS

Crystal Spring Publishing would like to acknowledge those individuals and agencies that gave so generously of their time, talents, and skills.

Bruce W. Muncy, photographer, desktop publisher
Lynn Davis, editorial editor
Dianne Smith, book designer
Nina McLelland Matthews and
Michele Lyn. Kaminski, copy editors

A special thanks to the Virginia innkeepers for the gracious hospitality extended to us during our visits and for their flexibility in accommodating our sometimes inflexible schedules.
Portrait of Bruce W. Muncy © Lynn Atkins
page 41, porch, © Beaurline 1995
page 81, exterior, © Beaurline 1995

A NOTE FROM THE PUBLISHER

As a service to you, we have compiled in the back of the book a complete listing of Virginia's inns. No one has paid to be in this list; it is for your use.

The pictured inns were selected by the author and publisher. Initial selection was based upon our firsthand knowledge and recommendations by travelers, other innkeepers, and the Bed and Breakfast Association of Virginia. These inns were visited by the photographer, author, and/or publisher before the final selection was made. Some inns were eliminated.

The selected inns agreed to pre-purchase some books and help defray the cost of color photography. Without this arrangement, an all-color, pictorial book of this size and quality would not be affordable for many consumers.

Although many fine Virginia B & B inns are not pictured due to space, we have tried to present a sampling of the different styles, sizes, price offerings, and locations. We welcome your comments.

Please mail all inquiries and comments to Crystal Spring Publishing, PO Box 8846, Roanoke, VA 24014.

FOREWORD

Virginia is the Mother State of the nation. American history began at Jamestown and Williamsburg. Virginia patriots sounded the call for independence. A Virginia son, George Washington, led the continental armies to victory. Four of the nation's first five presidents were natives of the Old Dominion. So were James Madison, the "Father of the Constitution," and John Marshall, the greatest of the Supreme Court's chief justices.

In 1861 those contributions almost came to naught. Civil war swept the land. At issue was whether the "United States" would exist in fact as well as in name. Again, Virginia moved to the forefront. It became the major battleground for the bloodiest struggle America has ever known. By 1865 and war's end, the proud state had suffered greater devastation than any other region in the Western Hemisphere.

Despite the stigma of defeat, Virginians rose from the ashes with pride. They created a "New Dominion" that is vibrant and prosperous on the one hand, traditional and historically minded on the other. The Commonwealth of Virginia thinks of the present and plans for the future to be sure, but it also seeks to preserve a heritage stretching almost 400 years into the past.

Few states can boast of its geographic diversity. In the northwest, the Shenandoah Valley remains an agricultural wonderland for wheat, corn, livestock, and orchards. Majestic mountains silently reach skyward in the southwestern quadrant, while meandering and picturesque valleys echo the commotion of progress.

The rolling country of the piedmont runs north-south through the middle third of the state. From its horse farms near the Potomac River to cash crops in the southside, this sector is a fascinating line of demarcation between mountains and coastline. The sandy flatlands of the tidewater retain an aristocratic flavor to the very shores of the Chesapeake Bay and Atlantic Ocean.

From "Little Switzerland" in the Virginia highlands to the fishing harvest of the Eastern Shore is a variety of life with at least some attraction for everyone. Highways varying from the breathtaking Blue Ridge Parkway and Skyline Drive to modern-day interstate expressways provide easy access to every site.

Virginia offers the widest form of recreational outlets. Hiking trails and riding paths, dozens of fishing streams, broad ocean beaches, mountain wildernesses, unforgettable scenery, two major amusement centers, state parks for boating and relaxation, plus the largest concentration of battlefields and other historic sites in the United States.

Metropolitan areas mirror 20th century progress. Yet in the hinterlands are small towns and rural settings that impart a charm and quaintness so often associated with Virginia. Visitors to any part of the Old Dominion will find a welcome — a genuine greeting of friendship, an open hospitality that has made the state one of the most popular areas of the nation.

The wonderful bed and breakfast inns that dot the Commonwealth are reflective of that spirit. Managed by people who care, the inns provide comfort, graciousness, a taste of the past combined with the charm of today. Such ingredients have made these inns some of the finest in the country. Further, these lodgings are verily the doors to Virginia excellence. They serve as appetizers for the historic and exciting feast the state has to offer its visitors.

This book — a beautiful combination of Bruce Muncy's photography and Lynn Davis's prose — is an eye-catching introduction to available accommodations located throughout a region whose role in the creation and progress of America is truly inestimable. *Bed & Breakfast and Unique Inns of Virginia* is the starting point to an unforgettable experience that awaits you in the Old Dominion.

And as we natives like to say: not everyone can be a Virginian by birth, but we always welcome adoptions!

James I. Robertson, Jr.
Alumni Distinguished Professor
in History at Virginia Tech

CONTENTS

THE COMMONWEALTH OF VIRGINIA

1. BLACKSBURG - Clay Corner Inn

2. BOSTON - Thistle Hill

3. CHARLES CITY - Edgewood Plantation
   North Bend Plantation

4. CHARLOTTESVILLE - Clifton, A Country Inn
   Silver Thatch Inn

5. CHATHAM - House of Laird

6. CHRISTIANSBURG - Evergreen
   Oaks Victorian Inn

7. FAIRFAX - Bailiwick Inn

8. FLINT HILL - Caledonia Farm 1812

9. GORDONSVILLE - Sleepy Hollow Farm

10. IVY - Guesthouses: Ivy Rose Cottage

11. LEXINGTON - Llewellyn Lodge at Lexington

12. LOCUST DALE - Inn at Meander Plantation

13. LURAY - Woodruff House

14. LYNCHBURG - Lynchburg Mansion Inn

15. MIDDLEBURG - Middleburg Country Inn

16. MOUNT JACKSON - Widow Kip's

17. ORANGE - Willow Grove Inn

18. PALMYRA - Palmer Country Manor

19. PULASKI - Count Pulaski Inn

20. RADFORD - Alleghany Inn

21. SCOTTSVILLE - Chester
    High Meadows Vineyard
    and Mountain Sunset Inn

22. SMITH MOUNTAIN LAKE - Manor at Taylor's Store

23. STANLEY - Jordan Hollow Farm Inn

24. STAUNTON - Belle Grae Inn
    Frederick House
    Sampson Eagon Inn

25. STEELES TAVERN - Steeles Tavern Manor

26. TREVILIANS - Prospect Hill Plantation Inn

27. VIRGINIA BEACH - Church Point Manor

28. WARM SPRINGS - Anderson Cottage
    Inn at Gristmill Square
    Meadow Lane Lodge

29. WASHINGTON - Sycamore Hill House & Gardens

30. WAYNESBORO - Iris Inn

31. WILLIAMSBURG - Applewood Colonial
    Cedars
    Colonial Capitol
    Colonial Gardens
    Liberty Rose
    Piney Grove at Southall's Plantation

32. WOODSTOCK - River'd Inn

28

Lexing

Shenandoat

Rt. 460

1

I-77

20

6

Roanok

19

22

I-77

I-81

Abingdon

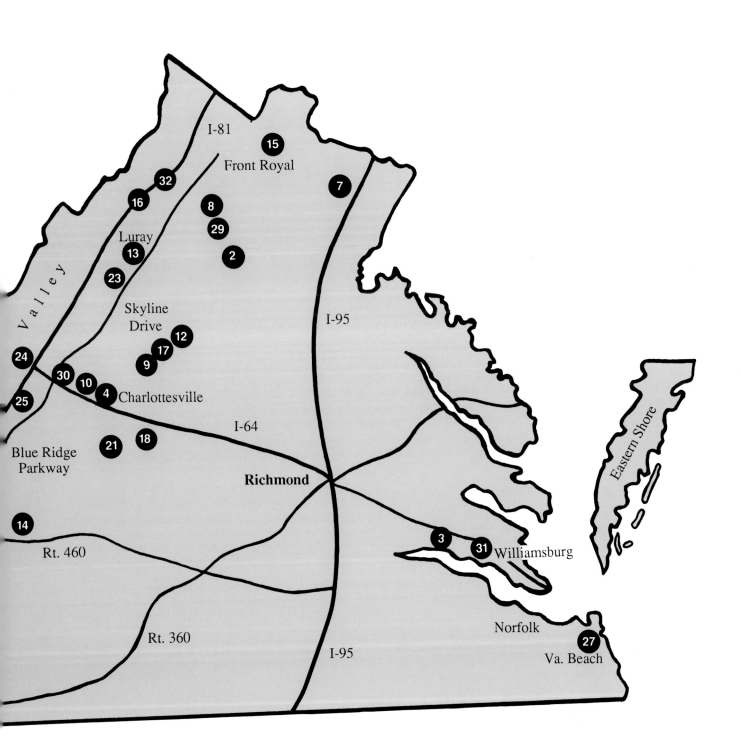

VIRGINIA
LEE'S COUNTRY

More than a century ago the beautiful countryside so typical of the Commonwealth of Virginia and many of its charming wayside towns were ravaged by the bloodiest war in America's history, the Civil War. Today many folks do not realize how devastating that war was to the state: more battles were fought here in the war that cost more Americans (70,000) their lives than in both world wars combined — which is why you will find the Old Dominion state peppered with battle sites.

Names like Cedar Creek, Hupp's Hill, New Market, Tom's Brook, Kernstown, Fisher's Hill, Front Royal, Five Forks, Fort Hood, Malvern Hill, Appomattox, McDowell, Cross Keys, Port Republic, Cool Spring, Fredericksburg, Richmond, Petersburg (whose brutal nine-month siege by Union forces remains the longest such occupation in American history), Manassas, A.P. Hill, Chancellorsville, Winchester, and on 70 additional occasions, Winchester. In 26 major battles and over 400 smaller engagements, more men fought and died in Virginia than in any other state.

Because no other state suffered such extensive trauma — the geographical position of Virginia right next to Union territory made it so vulnerable — we devoted this third edition of *Bed & Breakfast and Unique Inns of Virginia* to the legacy of 1861 to 1865. That war may have ultimately defined and solidified a nation, but it also left more than half of Virginia's men killed or disabled and destroyed countless family farms as well as such important cities as Richmond and Petersburg. The war-torn city of Winchester at the state's northern boundary, where Stonewall Jackson headquartered, actually seesawed back and forth 72 times between Confederate and Yankee forces.

Beginning with Bull Run (First Manassas), the first major battle of the war, and ending with the surrender at a farmhouse in Appomattox, 60 percent of the Civil War's battles was fought in Virginia. The Great Valley of Virginia had been the breadbasket of the Confederacy, until...

As described in the River'd Inn selection of this book, General Sheridan's famous telegraph of "The Burning of the Valley" that was sent from the old Shenandoah House in Woodstock boasted with awful accuracy: "I have destroyed over 2,000 barns filled with wheat, burned over 70 mills filled with grain and flour...made the Shenandoah Valley of Virginia so bare that a crow flying over it would have to carry his provender (food) with him."

In almost every B&B chapter in this book you will find some personal Civil War account pertaining to the inn or its community. There are mini-anecdotes and local oral history you will not find in published writings.

Some of the books written about the Civil War with a Virginia focus include *Lee and His Generals, Civil War Handbook, Civil War Trivia, Civil War Parks, A Treasury of Civil War Tales, Images of the Civil War, Insider's Guide to the Civil War, The Eastern Theatre, Jackson's Valley Campaign, Civil War Curiosities, More Civil War Curiosities,* and *Secret Missions of the Civil War.*

One of the world's greatest Civil War scholars, Dr. James "Bud" Robertson of Virginia Tech, who prepared the Foreword to this book, brought out a title in 1995 called, *Jackson & Lee: Legends in Gray.* He has written several other outstanding books: *Civil War! America Becomes One Nation; Civil War Sites in Virginia, a Tour Guide; and Civil War Virginia, Battleground for a Nation.*

Executive director of the U.S. Civil War Centennial Commission under President Kennedy, he had a great-grandfather who, according to family history, cooked for Lee!

Civil War enthusiasm has never been keener, with interest groups abounding. Many communities throughout the Commonwealth stage re-enactments of the battles fought in their locale, such as the May 1864 Battle of Cloyd's Mountain near Dublin. That engagement was the largest battle in Southwest Virginia. For schedules of battle re-enactments, contact the Camp Chase Gazette, P.O. Box 707, Marietta, Ohio 45750.

For a list of Virginia Civil War battlefields and markers, contact the Virginia Division of Tourism at 1021 East Cary St., Richmond, Virginia 23219, 804 786-2051. The Association for the Preservation of Civil War Sites seeks to protect and preserve important battle areas. It is located at 305 Charlotte St., Fredericksburg, Virginia 22402.

One of the best private Civil War museums in the nation resides at a tragic battlefield in the heart of the Shenandoah Valley — the New Market Battlefield Military Museum. If you haven't visited it recently, you need to, as the exhibits undergo change. In addition to all the wonderful artifacts, relics, and memorabilia, there now are maps of the May 12-15, 1864, Battle of New Market, where 4,500 ragged Confederates forced approximately 6,000 Union soldiers to retreat north out of the Shenandoah Valley. This was the last Confederate victory in the Valley. It was also the scene where 10 young VMI cadets bravely lost their lives.

In the eight displays on the battle are photos, portraits, uniforms, headgear, edged weapons, flags, personal items, weapons, letters, artwork, currency, stamps, medals, and more — that help tell the story. Personal items that belonged to Stonewall Jackson, Robert E. Lee, U.S. Grant, George A. Custer, and Jefferson Davis are part of the collection. The museum, which is open daily from March 15 to December 1, also shows a 32-minute film on the Civil War, and its bookshop has more than 1200 Civil War and military history titles.

Under the purview of the National Park Service are the battlefields at Fredericksburg, Manassas, Petersburg, and Richmond, which served as the capital of the Confederacy. The heartache of those turbulent years translates today into a bevy of other museums across the state.

Some "must sees" are Stonewall Jackson's Headquarters in Winchester and his home in Lexington; Robert E. Lee's office as it was the day he died at Washington and Lee University; Danville's short-term site for the capital of the Confederacy; Belle Grove, where General Sheridan holed up; the Warren Rifles Confederate Museum in Front Royal; and Hupp's Hill Battlefield Park and Study Center in Strasburg. In addition, Civil War buffs won't want to miss some of the Civil War cemeteries scattered around the state.

Legends of gray they indeed were — Generals Robert E. Lee and Thomas "Stonewall" Jackson, the greatest military leaders of the Confederacy but men who took no glory in war. Other great Virginian generals included J.E.B. Stuart and Jubal A. Early. Stonewall Jackson earned his nickname after the Battle of First Manassas, when General Barnard Bee of South Carolina proclaimed, "There stands Jackson like a stone wall."

Despite the passage of time, Lee has remained the supreme epitome of everything brilliant and gentlemanly. A leader of all leaders. A man for all seasons.

Virginians have a deep abiding love for those two heroes, as exemplified once again so clearly when Bud Robertson's book on the pair appeared in bookstores the end of 1995. At a book signing in Roanoke, throngs of people lined up to purchase a copy for autographing and in no time flat, the supply ran out!

As one Civil War re-enactor has said, "It's important to understand the Civil War era — the good parts and its bad parts. You do not know where you are going to go in life until you know where you came from." And, as historians like to remind us, those who do not study history are doomed to repeat it.

Some Virginians remember how their school teachers would refer to the war as "The War Between the States" — coming from the perspective, perhaps, that no war was civil.

With an extraordinarily rich heritage, the Commonwealth of Virginia has abundant, diverse offerings to keep any traveler delighted for days. What better way to discover the state's Civil War history than to make a circuit of Virginia's wonderful B&Bs.

TIPS FOR THE DISCERNING TRAVELER

Since our first edition of *Bed & Breakfast and Unique Inns of Virginia*, the Commonwealth's superb selection of inns keeps refining itself. You are hard pressed to find another state with so many outstanding establishments. Moreover, the proliferation of B & B inns nudges innkeepers to constantly polish their offerings.

In 1975 the first national B & B guidebook listed 40 inns in America. Today there are more than 15,000; nearly 600 of those grace the highways and byways of the Commonwealth of Virginia. The growth in B & B popularity is two-sided. More and more Americans desire the independence of "running their own show," so they become innkeepers.

On the demand side, escalating numbers of travelers seek the personalized services emulated best by such hosts. Once you have slipped back into a more gracious age and sampled the warmth and contented feeling that comes from staying at a B & B inn, nothing else quite satisfies.

B & B inns provide wonderful escapes from the pressures of life. They are a throwback to the times when Americans valued reliability, sincerity, goodheartedness, and the genuine desire to be of service.

Increasing concerns for personal safety also prompt more travelers to opt for B & B stays. Not only are the inns safe refuges themselves, innkeepers, often with valuable heirlooms embellishing their decor, find their clientele to be as honest as their own family. We have heard of only one innkeeper who lost something with a departing guest, and it was a copy of our book!

Like everything else in life, the cost of a B & B room has gone up. But the payoff comes when you find a nesting place where you can truly turn the stress button down a notch. The one commonality of B & Bs is that they are all different. There is no typical model. One of the great side benefits of the B & B movement is that it opens up more historical properties to the public.

Most B & Bs offer guests a place to lay their heads, a breakfast, and personal attention from the host. After those basics, a litany of creative variables gives each inn its distinctive character. Accommodations can range in price from $70 to $200 (fares often increase periodically), from a country inn with complete eating facilities to a homestay or B & B suite. Prices listed in the book do not include state and local taxes, and most are quoted on double occupancy. So if you are traveling alone, you might want to inquire if there is a lower rate for singles.

Homestays usually receive guests through reservation service organizations (RSOs) or B & B networks, which screen guests and match them up with what they want. In the process RSOs earn a 10 to 20 percent commission, and homestay hosts preserve their privacy. Avoiding any outward advertisement, homestays maintain a low profile to blend anonymously in the community.

B & Bs, unlike homestays, have signs posted outside their premises welcoming the world to their door. They also engage in their own public marketing efforts to attract business. B & Bs usually have more guest quarters than homestays, and some may offer dinner.

Inns, whether country or urban, often have a full-service restaurant and many more rooms than a B & B. Professional staff are apt to greet you at the front desk, while the owners themselves are usually on hand at the B & Bs and homestays.

Within these three main categories of establishments are wide variations, so you will want to check on details to avoid surprises that may inconvenience you. Few B & Bs accept pets, many are not geared up for babies, central air conditioning does not always prevail, some rooms share a bath, handicapped facilities are minimal, smoke-free environments are common, and bedrooms may not contain TVs or phones.

What you do receive at B & Bs is more than a tradeoff for these restrictions. The ambient charm of personal hospitality. Attractive furnishings with individuality. Hosts as interesting as their ample supply of reading materials. The caring feeling of home-away-from-home. A non-plastic, non-commercial atmosphere where you are truly treated as a human being — in fact, pampered. A relaxed atmosphere. The opportunity to savor regional and local settings.

Hosts respect your privacy, but make available their fountains of information as you so desire them. Many B & Bs will meet special dietary requirements if you give them some advance notice. It is always wise to ask about the check in and out times because they differ. Your hosts are often flexible but they do appreciate it if you let them know you will be delayed. While reservation and cancellation policies also vary, normally you must guarantee your room with a night's deposit.

You will want to book popular B & Bs several weeks in advance, unless special community celebrations or peak seasons extend the lead time even further. Although weekends fill up regularly, you most always are assured of weekday bookings if you get a spur of the moment desire to snooze away at a comfy inn. Unless specified otherwise in the book's listings of fares, the B & B accepts major credit cards.

Hosts open their homes for a myriad of reasons. It's a business venture or second career for some, who seek to fully earn a living. For others, they are part of a growing number of people in midlife who are parachuting out of high-pressure careers to restore their souls. The tax advantage of being able to deduct expenses is a motivating factor for some. To fix up properties and decorate creatively challenge many. Paying guests can enable a host to enjoy a lifestyle not otherwise possible — another attraction for being an innkeeper. But a common denominator underlies these fiscal matters: a love for people.

The B & B cottage industry is labor intensive and actually a way of life, so hosts would not last long if they did not enjoy meeting and serving others. Not unexpectedly, the hospitality of innkeepers is matchless and their B & Bs special, each with a charm all its own. Because of a rich historical heritage and unsurpassed outdoor beauty, the Commonwealth of Virginia has been well positioned to be a national leader in its B & B offerings to the traveler.

P.S. Virginia Tech helped to get the Virginia Division of Tourism on the World Wide Web. Check out this top-rated site called VISIT Virginia: http:www.VIRGINIA.org

This college town B&B not only pulls out all of the usual stops for friendliness and superb range of services, but complements its lodging with an intimate, 35-seat gourmet restaurant Tuesday through Saturday. You will find French service polishing off the sophisticated atmosphere.

Award-winning chef Jud Flynn, a graduate from the New England Culinary Institute and whose family once owned the mansion property, superintends the dining. A smokehouse on site sugar cures and hickory smokes the hams that are served in many of the breakfast dishes. Your innkeepers follow a century-old curing recipe handed down in the Jarvis family.

Besides their growing in fame Virginia-cured ham, the full breakfast comes with fresh fruit, bacon, eggs Benedict, grits, biscuits, and other goodies. A fireplace enhances the dining experience. The parlor refrigerator stays stocked with complimentary refreshments for guests.

Upon request, you can order a candlelight dinner in any of the guest rooms to mark a special romantic evening. Fresh flowers and home baked cookies in the guest rooms await your arrival.

The home, a hallmark in Radford's historic district, was built in 1905 by the Radford city treasurer and reflects the Queen Anne tradition. In 1993 the current owners purchased the place and restored the upstairs bedrooms for B&B quarters.

Although in a mountainous country setting, the home is only two blocks from Radford University in the heart of the New River Valley near the wide-flowing New River. Oral history has it that Union troops passed through on the other side of the river and shot a cannonball across the river into Dr. Radford's house nearby. The cannonball is still embedded

ALLEGHANY INN

there. The troops were on their way to Cloyd's Mountain to fight, where battle re-enactments still take place.

Guest rooms number five and are embellished with an assortment of antiques. An apartment suite with a private entrance accompanies a living room with skylights and includes a washer/dryer. A whirlpool enhances one of the queen bedrooms. For pure rest and relaxation you can seek one of the rockers on the wraparound porch.

The New River is sought by recreationists for rafting, tubing, canoeing, and fishing. Geologists believe that only the Nile River is older than the so-called "New," named by early American trailblazers who had not realized it existed. The river gets dammed at nearby Claytor Lake by Appalachian Power Company; the 4500 acre impoundment offers a state park, white sandy beaches, and a full-service boat marina. It is a grand place to fish for white bass and even flathead catfish and some crappie.

Your innkeepers can brief you on their golf packages and where to horseback ride, swim, play tennis, and more.

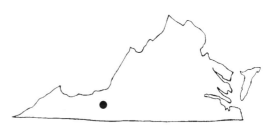

Fares

$85, $100+ for apartment suite, whirlpool room, credit cards accepted, night's deposit required, refunded with 14 day notice, book Virginia Tech football weekends and graduations early (2 night minimums then required), check in 4 p.m., out by noon

Courtesies

shuttle transportation, air conditioning, fans, private baths, conference facilities, refrigerator use, phone and cable TV in room, Fax machine and copier available, washer/dryer use, handicap access to apartment suite, whirlpool, young children welcome, pets are kenneled, no smoking

Lori and Jeff Jarvis
Margaret Jarvis Springer
PO Box 747, 1123 Grove Ave, Radford VA 24141.
540 731-4466, FAX: 731-1533.
From I-81: Exit 109 to Radford University onto Tyler Ave, go 4.4 miles, turn left onto Grove Ave after 7-11 Store, 2 blocks on left.

ANDERSON COTTAGE

*S*An honest-to-goodness country home amid a mountain valley of sparkling streams, this wonderful old place is truly reminiscent of bygone eras when central heat was non-existent. The original four log rooms served as an 18th century tavern, but with later additions they became a private home, a girls' school, and a summer inn, before belonging to your hostess' family.

Owner and hostess Jean Randolph Bruns has taken the rambling dwelling that has been in her family for more than a hundred years and lovingly turned it into a bed and breakfast inn, which she calls "a quiet place with plenty to do." Notable about the interior are the mantelpieces and some exposed log beams. In the absence of central heating, all the bedrooms and guest parlors have baseboard heat. The kitchen cottage, however, does have central heat and attracts skiers and winter holiday vacationers.

Jean's love for books and traveling is quickly apparent when you see her extensive personal library throughout the home. A former journalist and real estate broker, Jean often takes the winter months off to visit her son and family in Thailand.

The home features on the first floor a suite with a queen-size bed, bath, and parlor with a fireplace and private entrance. The second floor has a similar suite, accented with blue onion-patterned pillows. It adjoins the parlor room of wicker furniture, a twin bed, and red, white, and blue ribbon-patterned curtains. The other rooms are also upstairs. Guests often comment on a mid-summer morning how sweet is the sound of the trickling stream outside their open window.

The kitchen cottage, which is nicely suited for children and completely modern, has two bedrooms and baths with a living room, kitchen-dining room, and fireplace. It is comfortable year round. Furnishings throughout the

B&B include handsome antiques from Jean's family, moved out when she lived elsewhere and moved back when she set up her B&B housekeeping. Some good art adorns the old walls, where you will never find a right angle or straight line. Local pieces and a pre-Civil War quilt number in the collection. You can truly relax on the threadbare orientals because your hostess decorates for comfort!

Perhaps most inviting to the homeplace's many repeat guests are rockers on the L-shaped porch and in the parlors, where guests like to read and just relax. The backyard view comprises a stream from the Warm Springs pools, where children often frolic ("creek shoes" needed); colorful flower beds that get better each year; and aging shade trees. Her level yard is conducive for croquet, badminton, volleyball, and soccer. Indoor games, puzzles, and the piano are rainy-day pleasers.

A sampling of Jean's home cooked breakfasts might be turkey hash cooked with oregano and other seasonings; tomatoes baked with a dot of butter, basil, and crumbs; whole wheat rolls with spicy peach preserves; and fruit with vanilla yogurt. Another day might bring buttermilk pancakes with real maple syrup, sausage, and apples to your plate.

If you are a history buff, Jean can give you a rundown on the local history, the 19th century resorts in the area, and Civil War stories. She posts events of the region on a bulletin board and can also help you plan day trips. A short walk from her abode are the famous warm pools, bubbling up at 98°, and the Gristmill Square, where you can find some excellent dining and cottages of rural vernacular architecture.

The famous Homestead golf courses and National Forest trails surround the area.

Nearby are lake swimming, tennis, horseback riding, and some of the world's best fly fishing. You will never run out of scenic drives or picturesque hiking trails. And some of the nation's best chamber music is performed at the Garth Newel center.

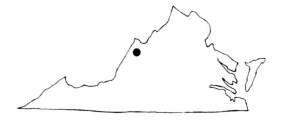

Fares

*cash or check only $60-$110
deposit is required, returned
with reasonable notice*

Courtesies

*fans in all rooms, refrigerator use,
full breakfast, no room phone,
TV special access, smoking in public areas*

Jean Randolph Bruns

*Old Germantown Rd, Box 176, Warm Springs,
VA 24484. 540 839-2975. From Staunton: Rt 254 W,
Rt 42 S, Rt 39 W to Warm Springs, past Warm Springs
pools, left at Old Germantown Rd (Rt 692).*

APPLEWOOD
COLONIAL

uilt during the restoration of Colonial Williamsburg in 1929 by the construction manager for his private residence, this brick colonial house showcases the best there is when it comes to architectural detail. Hallmarks include lovely wood crown dentil molding also seen in the Governor's Palace, H-hinges, brass door hardware, and Flemish bond glazed headers in the brickwork. The home enjoys a great location just four blocks or about one-half mile to the historic area.

The fireplace in the sitting room parlor has recently been enhanced with a walnut mantle and overmantle handcrafted by the owner. Guests enjoy trying their skills on the apple checker set on the signed Kittinger mahogany piecrust table or viewing "The Story of a Patriot" on the VCR/ TV hidden in the replica of the "Wythe House" TV cabinet. A basket full of menus personally selected by the owners and a guest phone are helpful with the big decision of which super fine restaurant to dine.

An apple theme accents the 18th century style interior design. Rooms are named after the botanical prints that line the parlor walls. Innkeeper Marty Jones has amassed this extensive collection of artifacts displaying the apple motif, including pictures, Franciscan apple china, a handpainted firescreen, and many other objects d'art. Apples were a natural item to collect for someone who grew up in Tell City, Indiana, named after the famous Swiss marksman.

In 1988, the owners rescued the house from college housing and opened the former guest home as a B&B. Its proximity to Colonial Williamsburg and the College of William and Mary has drawn guests from all over the U.S. and 23 countries around the world. Appreciative patrons have commented, "Your gracious hospitality made our vacation restful, your personal attention to making all dinner reservations was most helpful, and your knowledge on how to see everything in the area greatly expedited our sightseeing." Guests may choose among four queen bedroom, all of which have private baths and two of which accommodate children comfortably. The spacious Colonel Vaughn Suite has a sunny breakfast room, private entrance, queen-size canopy pencil post bed, and sitting area in front of the fireplace, which is banked by bookcases loaded with a large selection of books and a stereo/CD player. An innerspring sofa bed adds to the versatility of this quiet room, and a personal bath features tub and shower.

The Gilliflower Room, a large bedroom on the second floor, is perhaps one of the most gorgeous rooms you will ever find. Your hosts have captured the romance and elegance of years gone by with delicate lace bedhangings surrounding a high queen bed. The chaise lounge offers soothing relaxation after a day of exploring the storybook corners of Williamsburg.

Guest may choose among four queen bedrooms, all which have private baths

The dining room has a beautiful built-in handcrafted corner cupboard displaying colorful old china and apple teapots. Guests are seated at the pedestal table under the crystal chandelier to enjoy a full breakfast by candlelight. Afternoon refreshments include ice cold beverages during the summer months and hot drinks near the fire in the parlor during cooler days. Cookies and Virginia peanuts are ample.

In addition to the plethora of historical sites and activities, you may wish to enjoy the area's fine shopping or Busch Gardens for a change of pace. The nation's second oldest college, the College of William and Mary, is over 300 years old and a pleasant campus

to stroll.

As for the matter of reservations, you many want to remember that the B&B is booked way in advance for Grand Illumination, Christmas, and William and Mary graduations. All other weekends, holidays, or college events require a two-night minimum.

When not building mantles, Roger is a local physician and his medical advice and expertise have helped many guests while they are away from home!

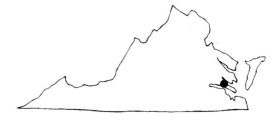

Fares

$80-$125, Jan-Mar discount, 50% deposit required, full refund with 14 day notice check in 3 p.m., out by 11 a.m.

Courtesies

free shuttle to train, bus, or Williamsburg airport; parking in front, air conditioning, limited refrigerator use, portable guest phone, young children welcome, no smoking

Roger and Marty Jones

*605 Richmond Rd, Williamsburg, VA 23185.
800 899-2753, 757 229-0205, FAX: 229-9405
2 miles from I-64, off Exit 238.*

BAILIWICK INN

$\mathcal{A}$n urban inn located in the heart of Old Town Fairfax, Bailiwick is only 10 minutes from the Vienna Metro Rail, with city bus service available to and from this subway system serving the D.C. metropolitan area and its suburbs. So you are well fixed to get around the area — whether it be for business or sightseeing Washington's museums, galleries, and monuments. And steps from the door is a bevy of quaint shops and restaurants.

Originally called the "Gunnell House," the federal style home was built of brick imported from England, laid in a Flemish-bond pattern. Inside highlights are a cascading staircase, fireplaces with original federal mantlepieces below the more recent Greek Revival influences, architraves positioned over each doorway and window, and a graceful portico.

Careful restoration has kept the home true to its style. Seven interior designers based their decorating work after researching the decor of the period. Outside, English gardens in the front and back reflect the era in which the house was constructed. Along with several other buildings in Fairfax, the house was placed on the National List of Historic Places in 1987.

Bob and Annette Bradley became proprietors in 1994 and carry on the tradition of maintaining the historic integrity of this unusually fine home, while seeking to provide a genuine, caring atmosphere for their guests that caters to their complete comfort.

Guests can choose among 14 differently decorated rooms, each named for a famous Virginian and appointed with antiques and fine reproductions appropriate to the personality and life history of its namesake. The rooms all have a small book library dedicated also to the namesake. Four guest rooms enjoy working fireplaces and two sport oversized jacuzzis. Twelve are bedded in queen size, three of which are topped with canopies. One room has two twin beds, and the suite features a king. Old-fashioned featherbeds, graced with down pillows, spread over the standard mattresses and box springs.

In the Thomas Jefferson chamber, you will find a leather footstool with writing desk that is an adaptation of Jefferson's famous "whirliwig chair." The mahogany armoire, dating to 1880, is referred to as "Beaconsfield" because it was made in that English city. Jefferson's portrait pictures him on the event of his second inauguration as president.

Superb French/American cuisine is served in the Belvoir Room, named from the home of William Fairfax and headquarters of Lord Fairfax during his early visits to Virginia. The three-course gourmet breakfast boasts a fresh fruit plate, a basket of oven-warm breads, two hot entrees, juices, and the rich Sumatra coffee.

Complemented by an impressive wine list, the four-course price fixed dinner menu offers gourmet dishes prepared using only the freshest seasonally available ingredients. The restaurant is open to the public five nights a week.

Bailiwick serves an English-style high tea afternoons to inn guests and the public on Thursdays and Sundays by reservation. Sweet offerings include its famous scones, served with marmalade and double devon cream, fruit tarts, madeleines, and an assortment of cookies and cakes. Tea savories are also displayed, such as brie and derby sage cheeses with crackers, tea sandwiches of cucumber and watercress, and country pate on a biscuit.

The Civil War left its mark on Bailiwick. The first skirmish of the war occurred on Main Street, June 1, 1861. Ex-Governor, "Extra Billy" Smith, a civilian, ran from the then Gunnell House to take charge of

the Warrenton Rifles. Their commanding officer, Cpt. John Quincy Marr had been killed, the first Confederate officer killed during the Civil War in a military engagement between the opposing forces.

Union Col. Johnstone was billeted here during Ranger John Mosby's March 9, 1863, raid. Johnstone, however, escaped capture that evening by hiding beneath the outhouse, wearing only his nightshirt.

Roof repairs made during the

1920s revealed Confederate military paraphernalia and medical devices and liniments to indicate that the attic had been used as a Confederate hospital during the war.

Fares

$100+, credit cards accepted, discounts, night's deposit, refunded with 2 weeks notice for leisure travel and 24 hours for corporate, reservations required for dining and lodging, a month in advance of fall and spring weekends is recommended, check in 2-9 p.m., out by 11 a.m.

Courtesies

air conditioning, conference facilities, access to refrigerator, phone in room, TV/VCR in sitting room, TVs available for guest rooms, washer/dryer access, limited handicap access, young children welcome, pets not permitted, no smoking

Annette and Bob Bradley

*4023 Chain Bridge Rd, Fairfax VA 22030.
703 691-2266, FAX: 934-2112.
From Capital Beltway: I-66 W to Exit 60, onto Rt 123 S (towards Fairfax and George Mason University), inn is on left at intersection of Chair Bridge Rd and Sager Ave, one block past 4th light and about 2 miles from I-66.*

BELLE GRAE INN

$\mathcal{S\!A}$ n authentically restored 1873 masterpiece, the rambling Victorian inn caters to the traveling business person as well as tourists. Its azalea courtyard is a picture perfect wedding garden and accommodates up to 150 guests with splendid pleasantness.

If that is not enough, then you must plop yourself down to sip a cool beverage on the wraparound veranda overlooking neighboring Victorian rooftops with the Blue Ridge Mountains in the background. Indoors you can sip a fine drink in front of the parlor while relishing the regal Empire furnishings of a bygone era.

Guests are greeted each morning with hot coffee, juice, poppyseed bread, and newspapers, followed by the innkeeper's fare of the day: waffles topped with strawberries, omelets to order, or eggnog French toast. Both continental and full breakfasts are offered daily. Accenting afternoon tea at 4 p.m. are tea, cakes, and brandy.

Innkeeper Michael Organ, a 10-year veteran training manager with American Express and then an instuctor at various colleges and training centers for 10 years, is the most accommodating of hosts. Southern hospitality rules here. But equally important, his dreamlike inn with its excellent cuisine is conservatively priced—one of the last of those great values.

Upon entering Belle Grae, you pass some mighty inviting wicker rockers on the gingerbread porch. This main part of the original building is brick, a prevalent building material in Virginia. The ornate, double-door entrance contains four striking, stained-glass panels in hues of purple and green. Engraved inside the crystal oval, the inn's name verifies you are at the right place.

To the right of the foyer is a lounge and formal sitting room. Adjoining is a small bedroom with private bath, one of 14 guest quarters at the inn.

Further down the foyer is the office area. Period reproductions, as well as antiques, are scattered throughout the inn.

A bistro, which goes to the outside courtyard, opens daily at 4 p.m. Dinner, served from 6 to 9 p.m., is available to guests as well as the public.

When you go upstairs to the other guest rooms, each with a well-lit private bath and nicely furnished somewhat differently in colors and fabrics appropriate to the turn of the century, lovely stained-glass artwork welcomes you to the alcove area. Nine of the guest rooms have queen beds, fireplaces, and comfortable reading chairs. Five suites feature large bedrooms with queen beds, reading areas, parlors with fireplaces, wet bars, color TVs, and verandas overlooking the gardens or the Victorian rooftops.

If you are in the mood for something really special, you may want to ask for one of the three bedrooms that is extremely large and comfortable, but oh so romantic!

Some rooms have antique beds with extra firm mattresses. There are canopy beds, Murphy beds, and sleigh beds. One room has a trundle bed that folds down. And if you have never bathed in a Victorian, claw-footed tub, this will be your chance. The bathrooms may be better stocked than your own, with such amenities as English herb soap, shampoo, moisturizer, toothbrush, and herb bath foam.

You have access to chess and backgammon in the sitting room, television in the parlor and bistro, reading in any quiet corner, and merrymaking in the music rooms.

Conceived and constructed by Martha Bagby, the wife of a local carpenter and craftsman, the home later was owned by a doctor for 50 years. His family of five daughters began the tradition of having

weddings in the garden courtyard or in front of the parlor fireplace.

Today pathways and footbridges connect the main house with turn-of-the-century adjoining homes—creating a neighborhood of restored Victorian architectural offerings, comfortable lodging, and a conference cottage.

Atop a hill in Staunton's Historic Newtown District, Belle Grae is named after two Mountains in view: Betsy Belle and Mary Grae. The Scotch-Irish, who settled the area because it reminded them of their homeland, named the mountains for beloved landmarks in Scotland.

The mountain-valley scenery continues today to be the magnet of this Shenandoah Valley town. Staunton is President Woodrow Wilson's birthplace and the home of the Statler brothers. Mary Baldwin College and Stuart Hall Preparatory School for girls are other focal points of the old, full-of-atmosphere hamlet. Belle Grae is within an easy stroll to shops, boutiques, and pubs. A mammoth antique warehouse captivates many a visitor. Walking tours

expose you to the local history.

Staunton stands in the hub of Shenandoah Valley Civil War history. It is equidistant from the battlefields of New Market and Monterey and the museums and burial grounds of Robert E. Lee and Stonewall Jackson. Guests also enjoy day trips to Monticello, Montpelier, and the Homestead of Bath County.

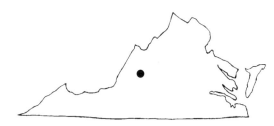

Fares

$60+, credit cards accepted, night's deposit required, refunded with 10 day notice, 2 night minimum stay for May and October weekends.

Courtesies

all rooms with private baths, air conditioning and fans, 11 rooms with fireplaces, conference facilities for 50, handicap access to restaurant and 2 bedrooms, not appropriate for young children, smoking restricted in parlor and dining room

Michael Organ

515 West Frederick St, Staunton VA 24401.
540 886-5151, FAX: 886-6641.
3 miles from I-81: Exit 222 onto Rt 250 W into Staunton, left on Frederick St.

CALEDONIA FARM-1812

he 1812 stone country home in Virginia's Blue Ridge Mountains, adjacent to the eastern edge of the Shenandoah National Park, offers views of the Shenandoah National Park from each of its guest quarters.

Host Phil Irwin, who calls Caledonia Farm "a most delightful and affordable experience," has visited 300 B&Bs in North America, so he has been able to learn from the best of the best. That translates into some of the most outstanding hospitality you will ever find amid first-rate amenities, beautiful scenery, a historical background, and abundant recreational opportunities.

Caledonia Farm derives its name from the mythological name for Scotland to honor the original immigrants to this magnificent area that resembles their homeland. Because of the dramatic scenic beauty, reminiscent of the British countryside, Caledonia's porches and patio are quiet favorites of travelers.

Your host is a retired "Voice of America" personality and happy to assist guests with their activity planning, as he knows the region well. He can steer you to five-star dining and other superb restaurants nearby. His working cattle farm in rural Rappahannock County lies within a two and a half-hour drive of 90 percent of Virginia's major Civil War battlefields, 45 minutes from 11 golf courses, a few miles from three wineries, and minutes from swimming, tennis, mountain climbing, and canoeing. You also don't go far to enjoy waterfalls, stables, caves, antique shops, museums, and performing arts. The first Washington museum is a mere four miles down the road.

The magnificent landscape was originally part of Lord Fairfax's 1735 land grants, and the manor house, second such on the plantation, exemplifies some of the finest masonry seen anywhere. The two-foot-thick stone walls, mantles, paneled windows, and wide-pine floors were beautifully restored in 1965 with the home's 32-foot-long beams remaining intact.

Along with a potpourri of antiques, Phil has on display for his guests a flintlock rifle used in the Revolutionary War by the original owner, as well as the first of the Civil War fragmentation cannon balls -- all unexploded.

Distinctive for its classic federal architecture, surrounded by stone-fenced pastures, Caledonia is listed as a Virginia Historic Landmark and on the National Register of Historic Places.

The Dearing Summer Kitchen Suite, an 1807 dependency, is ideal for honeymoons and romantic getaways. Its original cooking fireplace burns firewood yet today and the picture window views Virginia's prized Blue Ridge Mountains. Upstairs, where the house servants once were quartered, are a bedroom and full modern bath. The outside patio and breezeway provide a most relaxing niche.

On the second floor of the main house is another suite, which can accommodate a maximum of four guests with two private bedrooms and one bath.

Interiors reflect the 1800 period. All three guest quarters have air conditioning, working fireplaces, individual heat control, and super double beds.

Your gracious host takes pride in his breakfast menu including eggs benedict, custom omelets, smoked salmon, and other culinary specialties served at your preferred hour with candlelight, music, and unannounced extras to charm guests. An ABC permit allows for social drinking.

On the farm guests can pass time enjoying the spa, hayrides,

bicycles, lawn games, and strolling. Lovehearts take notice: Caledonia is usually booked two years in advance for Valentine's Day.

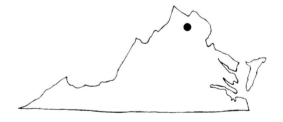

Fares

$80-$140, 50% surcharge for Sat. only reservations, first night deposit required, refundable less $20 if room re-rented, check in 10 a.m. to 6 p.m., out before noon

Courtesies

private bath in suites, conference facilities for 10, handicap access, not appropriate for children under 12, kennel 6 miles away, smoking restricted to outside, gift or business bonus certificates available

Phil Irwin

Calidonia is on the Internet.
47 Dearing Rd, Flint Hill VA 22627.
540 675-3693, reservations: 800 BNB 1812.
4 miles north of Washington VA on Rt 628. 68 miles west of Washington, D.C.

CEDARS

The Cedars takes pride in the fact that it is the oldest and largest B&B in Williamsburg. The three-story brick Georgian home meshes traditional colonial ambience with comfort and friendly service. It will surely set the tone for your visit into the 18th century.

You can walk to historic Williamsburg, "birthplace of our nation," in less than 10 minutes, and you're right across the street from the College of William and Mary. You can easily travel to Jamestown — the first English settlement, Yorktown — where the English surrendered to George Washington, Busch Gardens, and the plush James River Plantations. Steeped in colonial history, the region is a mecca of places to see and learn firsthand how America formed.

Guests at the Cedars may select quarters from among six rooms, two suites, and a two-story cottage that comes complete with a fireplace for the most romantic of getaways.

The third-floor Christopher Wren Room, largest of all with a splendid architectural openness, displays a king poster bed and gives honeymooners and anniversary celebrators cherished privacy. A dormer window with a window seat keeps romance in the air.

On the first floor, the George Washington Suite is enhanced by a parlor that receives streams of sunlight in the afternoon. Sporting an oriental flair, the Martha Washington Room has an antique four-poster bed that has been converted to queen size for the spacious needs of today.

The Patrick Henry Room, a refuge in a quiet corner of the house, charms its visitors with a fishnet canopy over the poster bed. Well suited for families, the William and Mary Suite occupies half of the second floor.

Floor to ceiling floral draperies define the Plantation Room, which is reminiscent of 18th century plantation life. You can rest your head upon the pillows and escape from the demands of this life back into the pastoral bygone days.

You will need to use the bed stairs to climb into bed in the Captain John Smith Room. The spacious and airy Thomas Jefferson Room, with an antique writing desk and wing chair, brings the inventive genius to life. Williamsburg yellow woodwork and Delft blue fabrics accent the interior.

All rooms in the house and cottage are furnished to spell comfort and pleasure. While portraying the colonial era, they do come with private baths. Some rooms have fireplaces. Eighteenth century antiques and reproductions fill the home. A distinguishing characteristic of the place was that it was built in the 1930s with 200-year-old brick from an old plantation house.

Candlelight and fresh flowers enhance the B&B's scrumptious, full breakfast spread out along the handhewn huntboard on the tavern porch. You might find oatmeal pudding flavored with brandied raisins or a smoked salmon flan, along with freshly baked bread and muffins and a mouthwatering fruit platter. Soft drinks and coffee are available in the afternoons.

The porch is also a good place to partake of a game of chess or backgammon. After a tiring day of sightseeing, you may opt to stretch out in front of a warming fire in the living room.

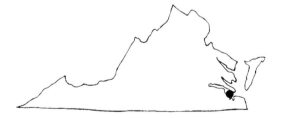

Fares

$95-$150 double occupancy, credit cards accepted, night's deposit required, 50% on stays of 4 or more nights; refunded with 2 week notice, 2 day minimum on high season weekends and holidays, check in 2 p.m., out by 11 a.m.

Courtesies

air conditioning, fans, off-street parking, phone on each floor, all children welcome, no smoking, no pets, gift certificates available

Carol, Jim, and Brona Malecha

616 Jamestown Rd, Williamsburg VA 23185.
800 296-3591, 757 229-3591.
From I-64: Exit 242 A onto Rt 199 for 4 miles, turn right onto Jamestown Rd (Rt 5 E), go 1.2 miles to The Cedars.

CHESTER

Nw owners Jean and Craig Stratton have redesigned the interiors of the all-time popular Chester B&B of Scottsville, near the James River. Previous guests will be elated to know that all guest rooms now have private baths.

Fireplaces, four-poster queen-size beds, oriental rugs, and large comfortable chairs in each room create an intimate setting, where you can relax amid luxurious comfort.

Freshly painted and newly decorated, all the interiors are spruced up for guests with an emphasis on comfort without compromising the architectural integrity of the 1847 dwelling. Jean, no less, is an interior designer, and she crafted Chester with an eye for classic elegance in both furnishings and accessories. Craig is retired from the Department of Defense, so the two high-energy hosts are well-traveled.

Departing guests remember "the beautiful furnishings, inviting warmth of the surroundings, feeling like royalty in the bedrooms, a scrumptious breakfast, and the delightful hosts."

Just a breeze down the road from the cosmopolitan, university city of Charlottesville, Chester presides on a hill of seven acres adorned by a century-old lily pond, immense stands of boxwood, and nearly 60 varieties of trees and other plantings.

A grand piano graces the common areas, along with more fireplaces. A well-supplied library entices everyone, while outdoor porches are forever inviting with their comfortable rocking chairs.

The Strattons pride themselves on pampering their guests — from the welcoming wine to thick towels, extra pillows, and warm duvets. You experience the fineness of a superb hotel enveloped in a private home.

The small country hamlet of Scotttsville takes you back centuries in time. The Greek revival home is unusual for the area because other homes built during the period were federal architecture. In fact, Scottsville has the third largest collection of federal architecture in the state.

The innkeepers will serve dinner for groups of six or more with advanced reservations, and they are well-equipped to handle small meetings. Chester's B&B guests also have access to good dining nearby.

Your breakfast treat satisfies any craving — fresh fruits and juices, homemade breads and granola, raisin French toast with Canadian bacon or a dish made with fresh brown country eggs, and coffee or tea. Elegant tables of white linens and fresh flowers add the final touch of class. You are fireside during the winter season.

The broad-flowing James River offers superb canoeing, rafting, tubing, and fishing. You can take in a croquet game or golf nearby. Hiking opportunities are ample, and downhill skiing at nearby Wintergreen beckons during the winter months. Chester is close to many of the focal Civil War points in Virginia.

In fact, Chester itself played a part in the last month of the Civil War during General Sheridan's occupation and partial destruction of Scottsville. In March of 1865, Major James Hill, the local Confederate Army Commander, occupied the house. He was suffering from battle wounds when opposing General Sheridan and his aide, Colonel George Custer, came calling on him. Thinking he was dying, they decided not to arrest him. Major Hill, however, ended up surviving, became a general, and when the Civil War ended he edited the Scottsville Courier newspaper.

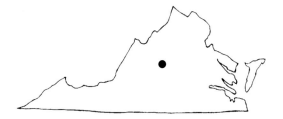

Fares

$100 and up, check preferred, credits cards accepted, 2-night weekend minimum during special local and University of Virginia events, night's deposit required upon confirmation, full refund 10 days prior, otherwise refund only if room re-booked, check in 4-6 p.m., out by 11 a.m.

Courtesies

shuttle if necessary, central air, fireplaces, private baths, one room with handicap access, no smoking , children over 8 welcome, honeymoon, anniversary celebrations with prior notice

Jean and Craig Stratton

243 James River Road, Scottsville VA 24590. 804 286-3960. Exit Rt. 20 S off I-64, go 17 miles, right on Rt 726, 2 blocks on left.

CHURCH POINT MANOR

The owner's extensive fine art and antique collection from his European travels personalizes this Virginia Beach B&B manor. Of awesome magnitude are two paintings that hang in the 20-foot-high conservatory. You will have to come see for yourself!

A restored 1860s brick farmhouse with a replica addition, the manor encompasses 10,000 square feet, with every inch of interior design beautifully executed by a professional designer. While the location is off the beaten track in a development that once was farmland — an historic tract at that, Charles I of England had land-granted it to Adam Thoroughgood in 1635 — the quiet neighborhood brings refreshing relief from today's bustling world. However, you are close enough to the beach if you want to venture out into the waves.

The local community has its own dash of color with historic sites. Next door is the old Thoroughgood House. Church Point was so named because it was the sight of the first Old Donation Church built in 1639 by Thoroughgood. In the 1920s, the land owners kept extensive oyster grounds and shipped much of their bounty to the Waldorf-Astoria Hotel in New York. In the 1930s, Lynnhaven oysters were trucked to the New York Stock Exchange, where they were routinely sold for $5 a barrel! Today, due to the dried-up beds, the dreaded MSX virus, and badly polluted waters, oysters command $55 prices.

You can trek farther and journey to historic Jamestown, Williamsburg, Yorktown, or Norfolk with its Chrysler Museum and Botanical Gardens. Fishing, sailing, and water sports are a seagull call away.

Church Point hovers over three acres off the Lynnhaven River, six miles from the ocean front and a half mile from the Chesapeake Bay, the world's greatest estuary.

tennis, bicycling, croquet, and a dock with canoe and rowboat. Golf and hiking are easy to come by. Thirty acres of parks and trails on the river front, with one trail leading to the Thoroughgood House, are practically out the front door. The manor is also right across from the $12 million Bayville Arts and Recreation Center.

You do not have to go far to antique shop, as some of the manor's antiques are for sale.

Owner Jahn Summs lives in Cape Town, South Africa, part of the year with his wife, Leslie, who lives there year-round. They have six children. Your delightful hosts on site are innkeepers Angela Craig and Peter Gagnon.

The original brick wall remains in the inn's breakfast room. If you grew up somewhere other than Virginia, you may not be aware of how older Virginians — the last generation is dying out — always called one room in their home "the breakfast room," a carryover from the olden days when they always served dinner in the dining room.

Also intact are the inn's original floorboards. The old root cellar has been turned into a pub. Ten guest accommodations, all individually designed, give you a wide selection. Perhaps the most distinctive, The Provence Room, is octagonal with windows all around. A center-draped canopy bed, fireplace, and high ceiling all contribute to a romantic atmosphere.

The Normandy Room on the third floor features twin closet beds, upholstered walls, and a ceiling in toile — utterly unique. Interior designer Nonie Waller of La Galleria used her own fabric creations throughout the manor. Faux paintings adorn many walls. The comfortable queen-sized beds may entice you to slumber forever.

You will wake up to freshly ground coffee, herbal tea, juices, yogurt, granola, freshly baked muffins and breads, fresh fruit, an entree such as Belgian waffles, pancakes, eggs Benedict or Florentine, baked French toast, and omelets with goat cheese and mushrooms. Punctuating your day are freshly baked cookies, teas, and fruit.

Offered on site are swimming,

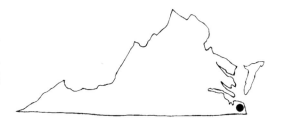

Fares

$100+, credit cards accepted, 50% deposit required, refunded with 14 day notice, check in 4-6 p.m., out by 11 a.m.

Courtesies

central air conditioning, private baths, fireplaces, conference facilities for 10-14, office facilities available, phone and cable TV in room, one room with handicap access, no smoking

Jahn Summs, owner
Angela Craig & Peter Gagnon, innkeepers

4001 Church Point Rd, Virginia Beach VA 23455.
804 460-2657, FAX: 460-2845.
From I-95 S: take I-64 E, Exit 282 onto Northampton Blvd, go 3.5 miles, turn right onto Pleasure Horse Rd, quick left onto First Court, 1 mile to Church Point development.

CLAY CORNER INN

lacksburg — home to Virginia Tech and its Sugar Bowl winning football team, the pioneering Electronic Village known nationally as BEV, *and* the delightful respite of Clay Corner Inn.

Encompassing three nice homes with uncluttered, simple elegance, the inn had been known prior as Per Diem, but the innkeepers changed the name because guests sometimes mistakenly thought the college town lodging was for government employees only.

The Andersons purchased the three-house complex in 1994. They acquired two adjacent homes in the fall of 1995. Their establishment lies one block from the Virginia Tech campus in downtown Blacksburg.

Their Huckleberry House was built in 1913 and will be open for guests by 1997 with four guest rooms, each with a fireplace. The cozy 1940s house off the back corner is currently a semi-furnished rental.

Guests appreciate the wonderfully relaxing atmosphere and are charmed by the warm reception of the Andersons. You will feel comfortable here.

When you arrive, after coming in from the brick-laid parking lot you are liable to see your hostess in her big red and green chair by the fire (if it is winter), pot of orange spice tea on her left, and her dog Solomon at her feet.

Sometimes you may need to ring the bell or just wander in and sign yourself in at the registration table. Your room keys will be there, and your hosts will catch up with you later.

You can choose from among eight guest quarters. The Santa Fe Suite in the main house has a Southwestern decor and features a queen bed, an enclosed rustic porch, windows, and skylight. You will find seashells, of course, in the Sanibell Room of the 402 Guest House, along with a king bed and white lace.

Recently refurbished with a new bathroom, the Sunshine Room in the 400 Guest House was named for Sunshine, Colorado, and is decorated in pale yellow with photos of the tiny mining town.

The innkeepers have used an eclectic mix in furnishing their interiors; they have emphasized "bright and comfortable." You will see traces of the Southwest intermingled with traditional and contemporary.

The usual breakfast fare runs from homemade maple pecan granola and dried cranberry meusli to fresh fruit juice, home-baked muffins and scones, and coffee and tea. On Sundays a hot entree, such as eggs Benedict, French toast, or baked oatmeal is offered.

If you want to make someone feel special, for $7 you can order a welcome basket, which consists of granola bar, soda, flavored seltzer water, candy bar, fruit, and homemade cookies with a handwritten welcome card on top. Fresh flowers are $6. On second thought, you may want to order those for yourself!

A real treat is the convenience of having a heated swimming pool on site, which is open May through September.

John Anderson is a part-time technical consultant, and his wife Joanne is a freelance writer, who specializes in restaurant reviews, so you will know who to turn to for dining suggestions!

Within a mile are an 18-hole golf course, tennis courts, and the very special Huckleberry Trail, well used by community and college walkers. The trail is also a safe place to in-line skate.

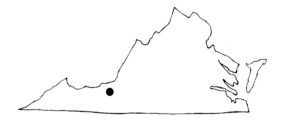

Fares

$85 for 2 on weekends, $75 Sun - Thurs, credit cards accepted, night's deposit within 10 days, refunded with 7 days notice, reservations 1-3 years in advance for holidays and special university weekends (including football games, Parents' Weekend in the fall, and graduation), check in 3 p.m., out by noon

Courtesies

air conditioning, fans, private baths, refrigerator use, phone and cable TV in room, washer/dryer available, smoking outside only

Joanne and John Anderson

401 Clay St SW, Blacksburg VA 24060
540 953-2604; FAX: 951-0541
Email: claycorner@aol.com
From I-81: take Virginia Tech exit onto Rt 460 (use Christiansburg Bypass), Business 460 into Blacksburg, turn right off Main St.

CLIFTON
A
COUNTRY INN

he Charlottesville area epitomizes sophisticated country living at its ultimate. Clifton, five miles east of the University of Virginia town, is one premier example. The interiors are magazine perfect, the surrounding environment has undergone a mammoth beautification program, and the royal treatment of guests is hard to beat.

Perhaps that accounts for its 1993 selection as one of the nation's top 12 inns and its international recognition in *Forbes, the Los Angeles Times, Conde Nast Traveller, Country Inns, Washingtonian, Southern Accents, Washington Post, Business Week, International Living, Glamour,* and *Southern Living.* Politicians and entertainment personalities frequent the inn — giving added luster to its reputation.

Clifton is on property that once was part of the original 1735 land grant owned by William Randolph. After his grandson, Thomas Mann Randolph (1768-1828), married third cousin Martha Jefferson, Thomas built the original five-room brick structure of Clifton for a law office. Thomas Randolph was a Governor of Virginia, member of the Virginia House of Representatives, member of the U.S. Congress, and son-in-law, no less, of America's third president, Thomas Jefferson.

The older structure built by Randolph reflects a federal style architecture; later additions and renovations were done in the colonial revival style. What is now the back of the inn was originally the front, which was terraced in seven levels extending down to the Rivanna River. The last addition was the 1930 double level, five-bay front porch with box columns.

Inside, the colonial revival style complements the simple detailing of the federal style from Randolph's day. The federally-trimmed fireplaces and mantles, locally milled pine board flooring in the older section, federal styled doors, and a faithfully reproduced staircase helped place the property on both the National Register of Historic Places and the Virginia Historic Landmark Register. During the Civil War, the home served as a refuge for Colonel John Singleton Mosby's family, after they were forced from their home near Middleburg. Mosby, the "Grey Ghost" of the Confederacy, visited his family at Clifton and sent them medicine and other necessities he captured in Northern Virginia.

Located on 40 secluded acres in the highbrow farm country of Albemarle County, the estate promises a 22-acre lake for swimming and fishing, a tennis court, spring-fed swimming pool with waterfall, and year-round hot tub. Those seeking leisurely sport may enjoy croquet and horseshoes. Guests do not need to leave the grounds to enjoy the Virginia foothills — the formal and informal gardens provide ample opportunity. However, if you like to horseback ride, your hosts can arrange that activity.

The common rooms inside are elegant, including the large drawing room, library, tea room, glass-enclosed veranda, dining room, and kitchen, which is also open to guests. English, French, and Belgian antiques decorate the rooms with Turkish and oriental rugs. American Indian photography, hand-painted botanicals, canopy beds, and chintz and silk fabrics embellish the decor.

All guest quarters include a private bath and woodburning fireplace. The small Carriage House was restored with architectural salvage, including bath fixtures, from the demolished Meriwether Lewis House. Set off with French doors flanked by windows on both sides, the outbuilding faces the croquet field, formal garden, and Rivanna River.

Inside, a loft bedroom overlooks the living room beneath a cathedral ceiling.

In the manor house and outbuildings are 14 rooms and suites. The Thomas Jefferson Suite in the main house features a spacious bedroom and living room furnished in period style. Beds are queen-size four-poster or canopied, all draped with soft down comforters. Lush premium towels dress the baths.

Chef Craig Hartman, graduate of the Culinary Institute of America and recipient of top culinary awards, prepares a delectable cuisine. He concocts fresh fruit fixings, homemade muffins, crab-shrimp omelets, Canadian bacon, and freshly-squeezed orange juice for breakfast. Afternoon teas, cheeses, fruit tarts, and just-out-of-the-oven cookies are served daily. For an additional charge, elegant dinners and a full bar, also open to the public, are offered nightly.

Clifton is a special inn for all seasons. When the trees lose their leaves, you can see Monticello, the famous residence that Jefferson

himself designed. Surrounded by such rich history, you feel as though you are treading on hallowed ground.

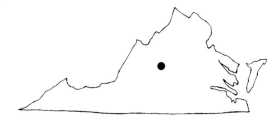

Fares

$165-$225, $100 deposit required, returned less 10% with 14 day notice, group and corporate rates, check in after 3 p.m., out by 11 a.m.

Courtesies

air conditioning, conference facilities, refrigerator use, concierge service, handicap access, children welcome, non-smoking environment

Craig and Donna Hartman
T. Mitchell and Emily Willey

1296 Clifton Inn Drive, Charlottesville VA 22911. 804 971-1800, FAX: 971-7098. From Charlottesville: 250 E, right onto Rt 729.

COLONIAL
CAPITAL

I n Williamsburg's designated historic neighborhood, this stately colonial revival home is three convenient blocks away from the heart of Colonial Williamsburg. "We're here to spoil you," rings the motto of B&B hosts Barbara and Phil Craig.

From their welcoming refreshments for arriving guests to the comfortable and tastefully created interiors, their accommodating manner serves you well. The little touches lend grace to your stay — nightly turn-down service, specially blended coffees, and a full cooked breakfast with a gourmet touch.

Antique furnishings, oriental rugs, and casual elegance invite guests to congregate in the parlor and breakfast rooms, which have seen visitors from all 50 states and 16 foreign countries. The large plantation parlor feeds into a screened-in porch, shaded patio, and deck. Its woodburning fireplace creates an inviting place to mingle with friends, old and new, during the cooler months. Air conditioned comfort makes this parlor and the whole house equally delightful in warmer months.

Five light and airy guest rooms with cozy canopied poster beds, (twin, queen, and king), ceiling fans, and private baths with luxury bath amenities promote gracious relaxation.

Individual decor in your room might include distinguishing features such as stenciled walls, quarter round windows and window seats, a private porch with rocking chairs, a corner sink, or an 1850s school desk waiting for you to send that note or postcard to a loved one.

Breakfast always includes fresh fruits, served with delectable ham and cheese soufflés, raised yeast waffles, caramel French toast topped with sour cream and strawberries that some have labeled "decadent," or sausage casserole with grits and fried apples. Juices, coffees, and teas are spread out long before breakfast is served. During the day you are offered a selection of award-winning Williamsburg wines, soft drinks, lemonade on hot days, warm cider in the cooler months, and other beverages. Colonial Capital has a liquor license, and brown bagging is permitted.

Parents of two and grandparents of five, your hosts are adept at making folks comfortable. Barbara is a former admissions officer for a women's college; Phil was a stockbroker and officer in a New York Stock Exchange member firm. Both are seasoned domestic and international travelers and sailors. Their resident golden retriever, Ginny, affectionately befriends Colonial Capital's guests and is skilled at positioning herself for beaucoup rubs.

Colonial Williamsburg, which served as the colonial capital of the Virginia colony from 1699 to 1776 and the capital of the Independent Commonwealth from 1776 to 1779, attracts throngs of visitors. The revered College of William and Mary is across the street from your B&B. Interestingly enough, the Civil War mostly bypassed the historic triangle of Williamsburg, Jamestown, and Yorktown, but earlier history abounds in the region.

In making reservations, you need to be aware that graduation, homecoming, and Christmas dates are booked at least a year in advance.

Besides a multitude of historical sites, you will find a host of other things to see. Busch Gardens and Water Country USA are fun, while shopping galore is to be had at the Williamsburg Pottery and over 100 factory outlet stores. The terrain around the inn is good for walking and bike riding ('get you there' bikes are free). Fine dining is everywhere.

A three story built in 1926, the inn displays a columned portico, spacious entry foyer, and columned side porch. Brick walkways completely encircle the main house and extend to the fronts of the two white dependencies, where lighted off-street parking is available.

Scene of small weddings and receptions, Colonial Capital Bed &

Breakfast evoked these words: "The essence of Williamsburg, hospitality... marvelous food...genial hosts...wonderful history."

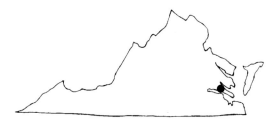

Fares

$76-$115, check or credit card, deposit required, refunded with 15 day notice, check in flexible, out by 11 a.m.

Courtesies

shuttle to Amtrak, bus, airport, conference facilities for 10, refrigerator access, TV with VCR in suite and parlor, well-behaved children over 8 welcome, smoking outside only, gift certificates and honeymoon packages available

Barbara and Phil Craig

501 Richmond Rd, Williamsburg VA 23185. 800 776-0570, 757 229-0233, FAX: 757 253-7667. From I-64: Exit 238 onto Rt 132, right at Lafayette, left at Virginia Ave to corner of Richmond Rd. Green three story house on right.

COLONIAL GARDENS

Formerly the home of the retired dean of the School of Law at the College of William and Mary, the B&B continues the tradition of gracious entertaining. Secluded in a woodland setting but merely five minutes from Colonial Williamsburg, the home blossoms with North Carolina rhododendrons, azaleas, and century-old oaks and poplars.

It was constructed in the 1960s using bricks from an 1800s courthouse that underwent demolition during the restoration of Colonial Williamsburg. Today, guests love to hunt for initials carved into the old bricks. Hardwood floors and crown molding distinguish the interior. A profusion of fresh flowers throughout the home carries the theme of Colonial Gardens.

The formal dining room, wallpapered with an authentic Shumacher Williamsburg reproduction print, sets the breakfast scene with china, crystal, and family silver gracing the banquet-size table. Unparalleled is the museum quality of the cutglass punch bowl, made in New York around 1880 and capturing the soft light angling from the three-tiered brass chandelier overhead.

Seasonal culinary favorites determine the menu, accented with gourmet coffee and fresh orange juice. Delectables might be baked blueberry stuffed French toast, fresh fruit cup, and link sausage. Afternoons deliver hot teas or mulled cider with gingerbread in wintertime. Lemonade, iced tea, and shortbreads punctuate the warmer months.

Some guests take their "early riser coffee" while rocking on the large front porch and visiting with Arnold the Overweight, the outdoor resident cat. The Florida Room provides guests with a place to relax on a cool summer evening. You can hear the low hoot of owls in the woods and sniff the mock-orange blossoms, while sipping iced tea and downing some of Scottie's home-baked cookies.

During the Christmas season, Colonial Gardens is elaborately decorated with Della Robbia garlands of flowers and brocade ribbon. Each guest room has its own Christmas tree.

Civil War history crops up in the library. Over the sofa is the long rifle carried by your host's great-great grandfather as a teen in the Confederate Army during the Siege of Atlanta. The library includes a large selection of classics, art, and travel books.

After a day crammed full of business, sightseeing, or playing golf nearby, you can head for the comfortable living room to pair off for a game of checkers on the hand-painted heart-shaped board, or opt to put together one of the puzzles, play your favorite tune on the piano, or enjoy a classic or Colonial Williamsburg tape from the nice VCR tape library.

Your innkeepers, Scottie and Wilmot Phillips, are transplanted Georgians. Scottie retired from 20 years in the medical profession, and Wilmot continues as an architectural renderer and accomplished landscape and architectural artist. You will notice his paintings and drawings throughout the home.

They furnished their B&B with a combination of family heirlooms and American and English antiques collected over the last 30 years during their travels.

The Rhododendron Suite is decorated in the French Empire style with Carrara marble tops, rich burgundy fabrics, and oriental rugs over warm, honey-colored hardwood. The Azalea Suite features a Charleston rice canopy bed and large antique English dresser with the unique feature of curved doors that must be opened before the drawer can be pulled out. Bright and sunny, the Primrose Room has a king bed and is furnished with painted cottage pieces dating to 1860 from New England.

Colonial Gardens' worldwide clientele remark that they do not forget the details that made them feel special, comfortable, and happy.

Fares

$95 for room, $115-$125 for suites, credit cards accepted, 50% deposit, refunded with 14 day notice, 6 months advance reservations needed for Christmas, 2 night minimum for weekends and holidays, check in 3-6 p.m. (notify if late arrival), out by 11 a.m.

Courtesies

shuttle from Amtrak station, fax available, air conditioning, fans, private baths, TV in library with VCR, children 12 and up welcome, smoking on porch only

Scottie and Wilmot Phillips

*1109 Jamestown Rd, Williamsburg VA 23185.
800 886-9715, 757 220-8087, FAX: 253-1495.
From I-64: Exit 242 A onto Rt 199 to Williamsburg/ Jamestown for 5 miles, turn right at Jamestown Rd, first driveway on left.*

COUNT PULASKI INN

One of the distinguishing characteristics of Pulaski's first B&B that sets it apart from other inns is the garden, which contains "memory" items given by friends. Their names are kept in a special register inside the inn.

The other uniqueness is the innkeeper, Flo Stevenson, who has lived in three countries abroad, traveled in 40 some others, and visited every American state. The daughter of an Army general is a conversationalist's delight. Before her B&B life, she was an administrator at the University of Tulsa, UCLA, George Washington University, and Brookings Institution. She has also worked in human resources with Computer Sciences Corp.

Her ancestor, William Byrd, built Westover Plantation on the James River and his son founded Richmond.

She has "done the best within her limits" to make Count Pulaski attractive, comfortable, and elegant. Her guests leave her notes of profuse thanks for a special, wonderful stay.

Each of the three guest rooms is decorated according to the name motif and has wall bedside lamps, night stands, crystal glasses, fresh flowers, a luggage rack, and a desk or work table. The American Room honors the original owner, a descendent of Elbridge Gerry, who was a signer of the Declaration of Independence, and features a four-poster, canopied queen bed. You use a step stool to hop in!

The Polish Room has a king bed that can actually be separated into twin beds. The crest beside the door represents Count Pulaski's royal family. Casimir Pulaski fought on the colonists' side in the Revolutionary War as George Washington's Chief of Cavalry.

The French Suite features a sitting room and queen bed. Lithographs of Paris scenes are Flo's from a trip there. Many of the home's furnishings, such as a centuries-old Byrd clock, have been past down in her family.

In the sunroom hangs a three-foot oil portrait of Count Pulaski and history books of the area and of the count, along with a collection of military patches, match folders, and flags. A bulletin board enumerates local activities of interest. The brochure rack steers guests on what to see and do and where to dine.

Pulaski is a mountain town in Southwest Virginia, with the New River and Claytor Lake nearby. The New River hiking and biking trail originates at the town's borders.

A Civil War reenactment is held the second week in June each year in nearby Newbern, where an excellent museum houses much Civil War material. A Civil War Trail Map will soon be available. On May 9, 1864, the Battle of Cloyd's Farm (or "Little Walker Mountain"), a few miles from Pulaski, resulted in many casualties and a victory by the Northern troops.

If you want to stay on the premises, a Steinway piano, cards, table games, and books can steal your time.

Guests have their fill of hot drinks, fruit, a main dish, and two sweet breads for breakfast. The English Toad-in-the-Hole is a baked pancake and sausage dish complete with prickly pear syrup. In season, Flo will dish you up fresh raspberries from her garden.

Guests are treated to candlelight in the formal dining room. Family silver, crystal, and fine china, against the background of soft classical music, add the elegant touch. For munchies during the day, the beverage center is always available, and sometimes you may find some cookies sitting out for the taking.

Built about 1910 of the finest materials by a meticulous owner,

Harry Roberts, the colonial revival home had been in the same family for 50 years before Flo purchased it in 1993. The gray-beige brick was made locally. Now on the National Historic Register and Virginia Landmark Register, the home has been undergoing extensive restoration.

American and Virginia flags grace your entrance into the B&B along with Count Pulaski's battle banner flowing in the wind.

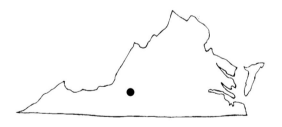

Fares

$60+, credit cards accepted, AAA discount, credit card to hold reservation, reservations especially needed for Radford College and Virginia Tech special dates, check in 3-6 p.m., out by noon

Courtesies

air conditioning, fans, private baths, fireplaces, refrigerator use, room phone available, TV in sunroom, smoking restricted

Flo Stevenson

821 N. Jefferson Ave, Pulaski VA 24301. 540 980-1163. From I-81: Exit 94 from N, 89B from S, 3 1/2 miles to town, right on Jefferson to corner of 9th St.

EDGEWOOD PLANTATION

The superlative romantic setting, Edgewood exudes opulence. Its richly decorated interiors surpass magazine covers! Exquisite upholstery, lavish canopy beds, gold-gilded frames, and lace and brocade window treatments accent every room. A Victorian symphony of sight — see it to believe it.

Deeply steeped in tradition, the National Landmark attracts the touring public as well as the traveler and often serves as a backdrop for weddings, anniversaries, and special celebrations. The host greets guests in full Victorian dress. Candlelight tours are sometimes offered at this historic home that has at various times been a church, post office, the first telephone exchange, restaurant, and nursing home.

This Gothic home was built in 1849 by New Jersey native Spencer Rowland. The land once belonged to Berkeley Plantation, the ancestral home of Benjamin Harrison, one of the signers of the Declaration of Independence, and U.S. President William Henry Harrison. During the Civil War, the third floor was used as a lookout for Confederate generals to spy on McClellan's troops when they were camped at Berkeley.

The 1725 gristmill on a creek yards from the house ground corn for both the Union and the Confederacy! On June 15, 1862, Confederate General Jeb Stuart stopped at Edgewood for coffee on his way to Richmond to warn General Lee of the Union Army's strength.

Today guests will see "Lizzie" etched on the window pane in one of the bedrooms, where Rowland's daughter died of a broken heart when her lover never returned from the war. Lizzie's Room, with its king-size, pencil-post, fishnet canopy bed, fireplace, and private bath, is one of six guest rooms in the main house. A magnificent 1790 carved tobacco-leaf bed, fireplace, and private bath reside in Sarah's Room.

Behind the main house sits the old slave dwelling with an outside

The Jeb Stuart Room has a massive queen canopy 1818 bed and sitting area with Victorian sofa and wing chair. An old "sits tub," private bath, and fireplace complete the picture.

The Victorian Room is site of a tall burl-walnut queen bed and sitting area with Victorian sofa, tea table, side chairs, and a great collection of period clothing. A private bath and fireplace add convenience and ambience.

A third floor suite has two bedrooms, sitting room, and bath. This spacious area charms couples and is also ideal for a ladies' group of four to six people.

Behind the main house sits the old slave dwelling with an outside entrance to two other rooms: Prissy's Quarters, a charming retreat endeared by a rose-covered, vine-canopied queen-size bed, sitting area, kitchen, and bath; and Dolly's Quarters, also with a private bath and a four-poster queen bed. The old slave quarters overlooks English gardens and the millrace canal dug by slaves in the 1700s.

Hostess Dot, who possesses an incredible talent for putting together the ultimate hospitable surroundings, will serve you tea lunches by appointment in the Tea Room charmed with touches of England. When the weather permits, the service can extend to the front porch and out into the gardens. Visitors are given hats to wear!

China, silver, and lace complement the flowers on the table. Scones, finger sandwiches, decadent desserts, and different teas mark the menu. Even Queen Victoria would be envious.

Your hostess, dressed in full Victorian garb, loves to give day guests a tour of the mansion. Her parties make for a special and different surprise when you are searching for a way to treat some

friends.

Edgewood is picture perfect for making a small wedding glorious and memorable. Package deals are available for small parties of six or less and include everything from the minister to the outdoor garden setting or elegant interior atmosphere where the bride can graciously descend from the double spiral staircase. After the ceremony, a Rolls Royce takes the couple to a quaint 1870s tavern for a delightful first dinner as man and wife.

As part of Edgewood's package comes a romantic honeymoon suite. The next morning the B&B's hearty country breakfast — with Smithfield ham, of course — completes the perfect beginning of the couple's new life together.

Edgewood will also cater large weddings for up to 120 people. Two gazebos grace the flower-filled gardens and make ideal "altars."

Dot dazzles her guests at Christmas with 17 ornamented trees. During the summer months guests enjoy the on-site swimming

pool. Surrounded by a wealth of other plantations unsurpassed by any other area in America, Edgewood serves as a good homebase for touring those properties.

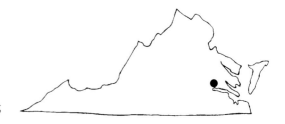

Fares

$100+, Jan-Mar discounts, deposit required, returned with 15 day notice, check in 3-6 p.m. (call ahead if later), out by 11:30 a.m.

Courtesies

air conditioning, fans, conference facilities, refrigerator access, TV in room, not appropriate for children or pets, smoking restricted

Dot and Julian Boulware

4800 John Tyler Memorial Highway, Charles City VA 23030. 804 829-2962, information: 800 296-3343. I-95 to I-295 to Rt 5 E.

EVERGREEN

ully called Evergreen The Bell-Capozzi House, this Southwestern Virginia B&B graces the hills of Christiansburg. Guests will be surprised that the house's lavish facade hides an inground heated pool in the backyard, replete with lounge chairs, gazebo, rose garden, and fish pond.

After a good workout in the pool, you can settle into comfort in a poster bed of one of the large bedrooms, each individually decorated with captivating works of talented, local artists. The Blue Ridge Mountain air doesn't always necessitate air conditioning, but central air pipes in when those dog days kick in.

Yes, there is a "Gone with the Wind" bedroom in this Victorian mansion. It features a king-size, four-poster bed along with a desk and tres comfortable chairs. Scarlett O'Beara and Rhett Beartler complete the makeup. Among the home's 17 rooms are five guest quarters, all with heart pine floors, original light fixtures, and private baths.

Fireplaces warm the two parlors. The formal library converts easily to a conference room that can accommodate 12 people. Innkeepers Rocco, transplanted from Corning, NY, and Barbara, a native of Virginia whose greatgrandfathers fought in the Civil War, restored and decorated "for comfort" the house without altering it. Guests call it "relaxed elegance."

Your hosts cook up a traditional southern breakfast with homemade biscuits, country ham, cheese grits, eggs, silver dollar pancakes, fresh fruit, locally-made jams, jellies, and apple butter, and growing-in-fame Mill Mountain coffee and tea.

Tea time arrives in style at 5 p.m. in the library during winter time with scones, cookies, cake, and small sandwiches. Summer guests are served on the porches, humming with rockers and swings.

Two blocks away are the Montgomery Museum and Lewis Miller Regional Art Center. The 204-year-old city of Christiansburg is the county seat for Montgomery County. Nearby Virginia Tech is a premier depository of American Civil War history and homebase for noted Civil War historian James I. Robertson, Jr.

Tech's Newman Library houses compiled service records of Virginia soldiers, thousands of books, letters, and artifacts, plus the recently acquired E.E. Billings Collection of more than 6,000 volumes and pamphlets.

When you're done scouting out the Civil War archives, you can canoe or raft the Little and New rivers, play bocce ball on Evergreen's lawn, fish Claytor Lake and the rivers, golf at Round Meadow or Virginia Tech, hike the Appalachian Trail and George Washington-Jefferson National Forest, horseback ride at Mountain Lake, or play tennis at several convenient sites. At Evergreen, when you aren't swimming, you can try your hand at puzzles, bridge, or the concert grand piano.

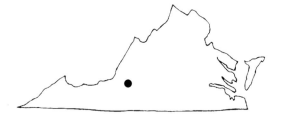

Fares

$80 (Mon-Thurs), $90 (Fri-Sun), confirmation with one-half cost, (graduation and football weekends/2-night minimum/ $125, balance due 6 weeks before arrival, refund given with 4 week notice), credit cards accepted, best to call afternoons/evenings, check in 4 p.m., out by 11 a.m.

Courtesies

Shuttle from Roanoke Airport, access to pantry refrigerator, phone in foyer and on each floor, TV in parlor-family room and porch area, not geared to youngsters, no smoking.

Barbara Bell-Capozzi and Rocco Capozzi

201 E. Main St, Christiansburg VA 24073. 800 905-7372, 540 382-7372 FAX 382-4376, Email EVRGRNINN@AOL.COM Homepage http://www.bmt.com/evergreen. 3 min off I-81, Exit 114, onto Rt. 11 and 460.

FREDERICK HOUSE

everal years ago a native son renounced the pressurized lifestyle of the Washington, D.C., area to return home to Staunton, where he purchased a cluster of three rundown ancestral homes and restored them to immaculate beauty.

Joe Harman, a former banker, and his wife, Evy, who had pursued an insurance career, have worked wonders with three townhouses. What was once a downtown eyesore is now an inn complex resonant with Greek revival charm and handsomeness.

The three buildings were built between 1810 and 1910. During the extensive renovation, more than 175 tons of debris were removed. New everything has gone into Frederick House, from the roof on down to the plumbing, wiring, heating, air conditioning, and security system.

Built in 1810, the Young House displays a Jeffersonian architecture closely akin to a home on the University of Virginia campus. Builders who had worked for Thomas Jefferson also built several homes elsewhere in Virginia. The Young House is probably one such home in the lower Shenandoah Valley. Joe's ancestors owned the Young House and the Womack House in 1895.

The Bowers House goes back to 1850. When her husband was killed in a train accident, Mrs. Bowers started a boarding house. She kept a cow in the backyard, where lavender now blooms in the spring and summer against the outline of a nostalgic, white picket fence. The Harmans, who live in their inn, also own a retail business and farm nearby.

They have furnished the inn with their personal collection of American antiques and paintings by Virginia artists. The interiors portray an elegant simplicity of old-world style. The appearance is scrupulously clean, the bathrooms modern, wallpaper and carpet smartly displayed. Greens, blues, and mauves in soft muted tones set the color scheme. The curtains and bedspreads are all coordinated. Beds are over-sized for sleeping comfort, and each room has bathrobes laid out for the convenience of guests.

A common room goes off from the lobby and contains books and magazines. Some of the 14 guest rooms have their own balcony or porch and private entrances. The Morgan Suite has two bedrooms (one with a queen bed and the other with a king), living room with fireplace, and bath.

For breakfast your hosts offer five choices of homemade specialties, all served with fruit and homemade bread. Afternoon tea is also available.

Frederick house sits in the midst of Staunton's walking tour. Your host can help you plan your sightseeing time. You are across from Mary Baldwin College and close to the Woodrow Wilson Birthplace, the Museum of American Frontier Culture, Statler Brothers Museum, and Gypsy Hill Park. Right next door is the YMCA, which Frederick House guests can use for a small fee. Facilities include heated pool, gym, weights, and other workout equipment. Within easy walking are enticing shops and antique stores. Staunton is one of the oldest cities west of the Blue Ridge Mountains.

Innkeeper Joe is a descendent of five Harman brothers from Staunton, all of whom were officers in the Confederate Army. One was killed at the Battle of Manassas, one at the Battle of Waynesboro. Two served as Stonewall Jackson's quartermasters, and the most notable of course, John, was Joe's greatgrandfather.

You are convenient to the Blue Ridge Parkway, Skyline Drive, Lexington's Horse Center and lots of outdoor recreational pursuits from golfing and canoeing to fishing and horseback riding. The hilly city is three hours from Washington, D.C., or Williamsburg, and two hours from Richmond. An Amtrak train station is only a couple of blocks away. Babysitting is available.

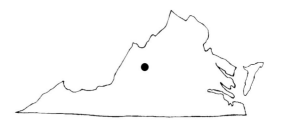

Fares

$65-$115; credit cards accepted, discounts for seniors, weekly, low season (Dec-Feb), business; reserve Oct two months in advance, reservations guaranteed by credit card, cancellations 24 hrs prior to 6 p.m. of arrival date, best to call 8 a.m.-10 p.m., check in 3 p.m., out by 11 a.m.

Courtesies

Shuttle to Amtrak Station, air conditioning, fans, private baths, fireplaces, conference facilities, room phone, washer/dryer use, children welcome, smoking restricted.

Evy and Joe Harmon

28 North New St, Stauton VA 24401
800 334-5575, 540 885-4220
From I-81: Exit 222, Rt 250 W, 2.7 miles.

GUESTHOUSES: IVY ROSE COTTAGE

I f you come to Charlottesville on business or for sightseeing, Guesthouses can open more than 60 doors for you! Ranging from historic properties to modern elegance, these B&B homes prefer to let Guesthouses handle their reservations and marketing. Prices start at $60 and go up to $200, from rooms to private cottages.

Some homes have been featured on the Historic Garden Week in Virginia tour, others are tucked away in rustic quarters with decks providing memorable views of the sun setting over the Blue Ridge Mountains.

Every home on the Guesthouse register has passed a rigid inspection using the standards of the Bed & Breakfast Association of Virginia and the National Network of Bed & Breakfast Reservation Services. They are located in town and country; a few are outside the Charlottesville area in Madison County and Nelson County.

Hosts are interested in your personal needs and tastes, so the more information you provide in making a reservation, the better Guesthouses is able to find the accommodation that is just right for you.

One of the most delightful B&Bs in the register is the Ivy Rose Cottage. It will remind you of Monet's garden!

Overlooking the Blue Ridge Mountains, lush pastures, and the Mechums River Valley, charming Ivy Rose will captivate your heart.

The cottage is located in Ivy, halfway between Shenandoah National Park and Charlottesville, home of the University of Virginia. Stonewall Jackson's troops were entrained on this beautiful acreage and in the Mechums River Valley below during the Shenandoah Campaign.

Ivy Rose has a steep roof and is handbuilt of cypress in a mixed Victorian-Gothic design by your talented hosts, who used many architectural treasures.

Copper trellis work and pergolas surround the enchanting structure with climbing roses and wisteria — giving guests a sense of old-world charm. You find yourself encircled in a calming gardenland sanctuary, highlighted by an enticing antique rose garden that is encompassed by perennial flowerbeds.

Eight acres of other colorful flowers, azaleas, ivy, roses, and blooming trees cover the property.

The romance of this cozy, private place you can call your own, is carried room to room in a tasteful blend of warm-hued woods and fine antiques. The double drawing room combines a sitting area and delightful bedroom with a queen-size hand-wrought iron bed. There, guests can enjoy the bedside warmth of a wonderful gas-log stove.

Off this bedroom, guests can relax in an entrancing greenhouse with wicker furniture and stained glass. Adjoining the greenhouse is a kitchenette and bathroom facilities.

The romantically-inclined will be enthralled with the upstairs — a vary magical honeymoon suite, complete with Romeo balcony and half-bath. You will find the unique rooms of this fascinating place graced with timeless panoramic photos, beautiful furniture, and fragrant bouquets from your hosts numerous gardens.

A special treat welcomes arriving guests. For breakfast, you enjoy a gourmet menu of soufflés, fresh baked scones and muffins, or a variety of other delectables. Fresh herbs, edible flowers and berries from the owners' seasonal fruit and vegetable gardens garnish your plate.

You will want to make time to see the earthenware pottery studio and gallery on the property. Your hostess makes lovely hand-thrown floral pottery. You'll find many of her art pieces accenting the inn.

Other activities nearby include golf, hiking, fishing, boating, horseback riding, and visiting the many area wineries. Carriage and balloon rides can be arranged.

Many guests visit Ivy Rose to celebrate special events. Once you've discovered this incredible niche, you'll find it hard to leave and will want to return. The warm ways of your hosts in such a place of exceptional beauty leave an indelible impression.

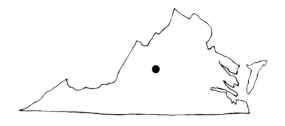

Fares

$150-$200, check or credit card for deposit, balance by cash or check, deposit refunded with 7 day notice, minus $15

Courtesies

ceiling fans, window air conditioners, TV, smoking limited to outdoors

Guesthouses: Mary Hill Caperton

PO Box 5737, Charlottesville, VA 22905.
804 979-7264, FAX 804 293-7792.

HIGH MEADOWS VINEYARD & MOUNTAIN SUNSET INN

The personal reward of sharing Virginia's prize bed and breakfasts with you and others since our First Edition is noting the good inns that have gotten even better in their maturity. Your wonderful hosts, Peter Sushka and Mary Jae Abbitt, are proud to show off their newly renovated Mountain Sunset Queen Anne Manor House that overlooks grand mountain panoramas, the 750 Pinot Noir grapevines planted on some mighty fertile land, and the music room converted into an additional bedroom with a two-person jacuzzi.

Eleven years ago, in their search for an historic dwelling to make into a country inn, Peter and Jae stumbled upon a newspaper ad touting High Meadows Inn as a "restoration gem." What they found has turned out to be the only structure of its type in the state — a federalist-Victorian style of architecture — and easily made its way onto the National Historic Register and Virginia Historic Landmark Register.

Moreover, in a matter of a few short years they have cultivated a vineyard that yields the most per acre of Pinot Noir in the Commonwealth with 3 1/2 tons of grapes an acre. Guests, of course, count among the beneficiaries during the twilight ritual of tasting three to four wines, accompanied with a platter of savory hors d'oeuvres. Grape harvest weekends have become the most popular times to visit High Meadows.

One of Virginia's scenic byways, the Constitution Route, passes the hilltop country inn of 50 acres and is named for Thomas Jefferson and the framers of the Constitution who lived and regularly traveled on this lovely dogwood-etched road.

The federalist portion of High Meadows was built in 1832, the Victorian part in 1882, and a Queen Anne style companion inn in 1905. A bi-level longitudinal hall connects the two oldest sections. Altogether there are 17 rooms and nine fireplaces, restored entirely by the hands of the proprietor innkeepers who were able to keep the original grained woodwork intact. High Meadows, in fact, is one of the few honestly restored inns in the state.

Seven spacious bedrooms and six suites, each with a private bath, accommodate guests, and are arranged with period-perfect antiques, original and antique art that include botanicals and steel engravings, festoon curtains, porcelain Lladros, and oriental rugs. Sitting and writing areas provide guests with some spreading out space, and a decanter of port or sherry completes the picture. Fresh flowers, fruits, cookies, and candy are provided in the main common rooms.

The Cabernet 'n Cream Suite features a private sunporch, queen canopy bed, and two-person soaking tub next to a working fireplace. Beautifully decorated in cabernet wine and creme colors, the room comes upon request with a bottle of cabernet sauvignon, of course! In the 1832 portion of the inn, the Surveyor's Suite, endowed with a queen brass bed, opens up to a private porch and sitting room with loveseats around a working fireplace.

Special offerings at High Meadows include the four and six course dinners served by candlelight Friday, Saturday, and Sunday ($25 - $40 per person), and the unique European evening supper baskets offered weeknights ($50 per couple).

Fresh herbs and vegetables, local shiitake mushrooms, cheeses, and fine local and French wines complement the delectable weekend fare, but more than just food appears in your weeknight basket. You are apt to find some roses, a book of poetry, or some choice surprise. Guests may invite others to join them for meals, often in a soft atmosphere of quiet, live music.

Breakfast is laid out with freshly squeezed orange juice, lots of homemade breads, fresh fruit, gourmet egg dishes, and beverages.

Guests are free to roam the antique rose and flower gardens, vineyards, and footpaths to the two ponds and trickling creeks, where you can enjoy duck and bird watching. There is nothing as inviting as the picturesque gazebo, nestled among dogwoods, holly trees, and yellow Scotch Broom.

Your location could not be more convenient for touring Jefferson's Monticello as well as the other presidential homes of Monroe and Madison, visiting the University of Virginia, sampling wineries, lunching at Michie Tavern, canvassing the autumn colors of the Blue Ridge, strolling the National Register town of Scottsville, and "antiquing."

High Meadows is also in a good spot for enjoying the outdoors. The old time Hatton Ferry is a novelty for sure, while canoeing, tubing, and fishing on the close-by James River also make for memories not easily forgotten — as the more than 15,000 High Meadows guests will attest.

Says Jae, "We try to offer our guests tranquil moments away from the stress of life." Peter, since retiring as a U. S. Navy nuclear submarine officer, opened High Meadows to weekday traffic in 1988, and utters words of satisfaction regarding innkeeping: "The parting warm smiles and repeat guests such as the family that has returned 22 times make the efforts worth it."

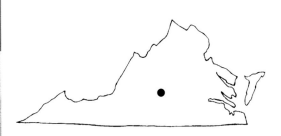

Fares

$85-$165, one night deposit required, returned with 10 day notice, check in 4 p.m., out by 11 a.m., 2 night minimum in spring, fall, and all holidays

Courtesies

air conditioning, fans, conference facilities, refrigerator use, washer/dryer access, 1 room with handicap access, children welcome, pets permitted, smoking restricted

Peter Sushka and Mary Jae Abbitt, Chef and Owners/Hosts

High Meadows Lane, Scottsville VA 24590. 800 232-1832, 804 286-2218, FAX: 286-2124 From I-64: Exit 121 (Monticello) onto Rt 20 S. Go 17 miles, cross Rt 726 (James River Rd), 3/10 mile further, inn on left at High Meadows Lane.

HOUSE OF LAIRD

any B&Bs personify elegance, but the House of Laird actually reaches a unique elevation in its beautifully designed, sculptured-like interiors. It was an unusually gifted eye that made such perfect use of space, proportion, and balance to create the magnificent, beyond improvement, decor. Everything just goes together so well you wonder what you have stumbled upon.

And in Chatham, no less! Actually one of the oldest towns in Virginia, but far enough away from developed metropolitan and population areas that tourists have not yet found this gem. No convention bureau touts its attractions or markets its wares. But if you want to sample a non-harried life-style, where the harshness of modern life has not intruded on the gentleness of its people, then come to the peace and quiet of this Southside town. Its people are content with their simple way of life, still value honesty and forthrightness, and help out one another in neighborly friendliness that seems to have disappeared elsewhere.

Owned by the same large family until the Lairds purchased it, this century-old Greek revival home with four massive exterior columns spawned four generations that recall fond memories of extended summer visits. The house fronts on Main Street, which is a classic portrait of Old America, U.S.A., where wonderfully seasoned residences line both sides of the street with nostalgic dignity. A grove of ancient oaks and gardens surrounds the home, whose architectural design of four rooms over four, separated with a central hall that connects to a kitchen at the rear, lends itself well for a bed and breakfast.

One guest quarters, the Library Suite, is graced with two fireplaces, fully-stocked library and queen-size bed, an exact copy of a Sheraton painted bed at Hamwood Estate in County Meath, Ireland. The exquisite four-poster canopy is made of mahogany.

Family pieces, including a century-old Empire bed with canopy, supply comforts to those staying in the Empire Room, which is hallmarked by the superb imported draperies and hand-screened wallpaper in the bath. Shades of muted pink and contours softened by curved decorative pieces make this room a favorite of honeymooners and anniversary couples.

It is so obvious that every detail at the House of Laird has been carefully planned and executed with the precision of a skilled craftsperson. The professionally restored and decorated efforts more than do justice to the classical balance of the 1880 home. Breathtaking antiques, fine reproductions, fireplaces in every room, imported fabrics, rugs, and moldings could not be better.

The dining room, as indeed the entire home, could walk away with national design honors. Breakfast itself is in the same creative league: freshly-blended fruit juice, bowl of in-season fruit, sausage crepes (made of sausage, cheddar and feta cheeses enveloped in a thin crepe and covered with a delectable sauce of baked apples and raisins), freshly-baked breads, cereals, and beverages.

A snack bar is always open to satisfy guests with cheese, fruit, nuts, chips, bottled waters, and sodas. If you haven't already suspected from the meticulously selected furnishings, your innkeepers are avid antique collectors and travelers. They love to entertain, and Mrs. Laird possesses an enviable collection of teddy bears. Her baking skills have won numerous ribbons at the Virginia State Fair.

If for no other reason than to stay over in this lovely home, it is worth a trip to Chatham. However, you will probably fall in love with the quiet, little town where people still sit on their front porches and

have time for one another. The county seat for Pittsylvania County and the home of Chatham Hall School for Girls and Hargrave Military Academy, the town was named after William Pitt, first Earl of Chatham, who sided with the American revolutionaries and against the crown.

As one couple so aptly summarized their experience at the House of Laird — "We will treasure the time forever. We were made to feel like a king and queen...in the peaceful and quiet surroundings of elegance and the royalty of a mansion, yet the comfort and warmth of home. Your special touches made our stay so wonderful...the luggage carried to our room, garden flowers in vases, heated towels in the beautiful bath. This rare jewel sparkles in every respect!"

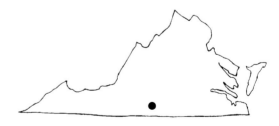

Fares

$95 + - $135 +, a deposit required, refunded with 7 day notice, check in 3-7 p.m., out by 11 am. Two night minimum stay on weekends.

Courtesies

air conditioning, fans, private bath, phone, TV in room, washer/dryer access, handicap access, children over 12 welcome, smoking restricted

Mr. and Mrs. Ed Laird

PO Box 1131, Chatham VA 24531. 800 201-7335. From Rt 29: Chatham exit to Business 29/Main St, 335 S Main.

INN AT
GRISTMILL
SQUARE

eading, well-known personalities sometime frequent Virginia's tasteful inns, and that spurred one Gristmill guest to comment upon departure that she enjoyed her stay at the inn, especially the extra treat of dining next to a famous person.

Gristmill Square, like a quaint village unto itself, opened to bed and breakfast visitors in 1972, although the Waterwheel Restaurant in the old mill has been serving guests since 1970. The entire complex comprises five restored buildings built in the 1800s around a courtyard. At various times these buildings were formerly a hardware store, blacksmith shop, mill, and two private residences.

Since 1771 there has been a mill on the Warm Spring Run site. It is listed as a National and a Virginia Historic Landmark. Today the old blacksmith shop houses the Country Stores, while guest quarters fill six rooms in the former hardware store and four units in one of the old homes, the Steel House.

An anecdotal story relates that the first mill was built by Simon Kenton for Jacob Butler. Born in 1755 in the Tidewater region of Virginia, Kenton fled his home at the age of 16 after fighting a rival for the girl he loved and thinking he had killed the young man.

Last to be restored, the Miller House offers the Oat, Barley, Rye, and Wheat rooms to travelers. Also on the inn's premises are the Simon Kenton Pub, the Bath and Tennis club with its three tennis courts that look out to mountain vistas, a swimming pool, and sauna.

Each room at Gristmill Square, smartly tailored and spanking clean, retains a distinctive air. Most are large and some come paired; a few have canopy beds, fireplaces, and kitchens, and a jacuzzi enhances one. Each room comes with cable TV, phone, hair dryer, small refrigerator and private bath.

Your continental breakfast is delivered when you want it, or placed in the suites with kitchens the night before. A fire is laid daily in each fireplace, with extra logs by the hearth. You may opt to eat dinner or Sunday brunch at the Waterwheel Restaurant, where a chef whips up continental and American cuisine and serves a tasty local trout, one of nature's best foods in these days of low cholesterol diets. Patrons may select their own wine from the wine cellar next to the mill stream.

The McWilliams, your innkeepers, ran a country inn in Vermont before picking up stakes for similar terrain in the South. Mr. McWilliams, a graduate of the Cornell Hotel School, died in 1985, so his son Bruce has since been the manager.

Located in spa country, this rural Allegheny Mountain retreat lies one mile from the Warm Springs pools which give the tiny town of 250 population its name, Warm Springs. These refreshing, unspoiled pools, always a steady 98°, open each day at 9 a.m. and close at 6 p.m.

Miles and miles of recreational forests, which provide abundant opportunities for horseback riding, fishing, hunting, and hiking, encircle this enclave. Championship golf courses at The Homestead are a mere 20 minutes down the road. Homestead day and night skiing during the winter months offers families many memories of fun. The Homestead, by the way, is one of the best places in the nation to learn how to ski.

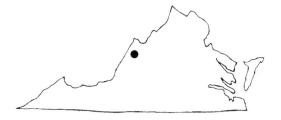

Fares

$80-$160 for European Plan, $155-$210 for Modified American Plan that also includes five-course dinner and gratuities, deposit required, refunded with 5 day notice, check in 2 p.m., out by noon

Courtesies

shuttle by arrangement, air conditioning in rooms, conference facilities for 40, children welcome, smoking restricted in dining room.

The McWilliams Family

Box 359, Rt 645, Warm Springs VA. 24484. 540 839-2231, FAX: 839-2231. From Rt 220 turn onto Rt 619, then Rt 645.

INN AT MEANDER PLANTATION

You return to a gentler time when you come upon The Inn at Meander Plantation. North of Orange, the 1766 columned mansion is cradled in the heart of Jefferson's Virginia. This is colonial living at its best.

The historic country estate gives you the ultimate restful escape to the pleasures of a simpler life. Lovely old boxwood gardens frame the imposing manor house, while wildlife abounds in the sprawling fields and woods.

You have serene places to stroll and will even see bluebirds flitter from post to post. Horses graze on the knoll. The grounds offer croquet and volleyball, while the country lanes beckon bikers. You may want to stake out the hammock that offers stunning views of the Blue Ridge Mountains, or opt for the white rockers on porches in the back.

Col. Joshua Fry, a surveyor partner with Thomas Jefferson's father, Peter, patented the plantation in 1726. Fry, who drew the first official map of Virginia, commanded the Virginia forces in the French and Indian War; George Washington was his second in command!

Fry's son, Henry Fry, Sr., built the first manor house on the property in 1766, and it was a frequent stopover for Thomas Jefferson on his way to Monticello.

During the Civil War, Robert E. Lee rested in the shade of a sycamore at a corner of the land while a local blacksmith shod his horse. Confederate troops crossed the nearby Robinson River en route to the Battle of Cedar Mountain. Today you can tube down that river.

Inside the house, guests can sit in the parlor and think what it was like when Jefferson discoursed there with General Lafayette. Private nooks for reading abound. A baby grand piano is always ready for a willing musician.

Lots of sun pours into the country mansion for a cheerful atmosphere. During the sleep hours you slip under down comforters onto lush pillows on four poster queen beds. Antiques and period reproductions fill the eight guest rooms, all finely decorated and with private baths.

The full country gourmet breakfast is served in the formal dining room and in nice weather under the arched breezeway. Freshly baked breads and muffins topped with homemade apple butter or fruit preserves compliment the creative and seasonal entrees.

Heart healthy breakfasts are available upon request. Innkeeper Suzie Blanchard, a food writer/teacher/enthusiast, freely shares her culinary knowledge and recipes. Her cookbook collection spills over 300 volumes.

With advance reservations, guests can have dinner. If you embark on a sightseeing excursion, you might want to request a picnic basket.

From the inn you can easily visit Central Virginia's many attractions — Montpelier, home of James and Dolley Madison; Shenandoah National Park; Thomas Jefferson's Monticello, Ash Lawn, and Michie Tavern; Charlottesville and the University of Virginia.

Much Civil War action occurred in the nearby countryside at Cedar Mountain, Chancellorsville, and Wilderness and Brandy Station Battlefields.

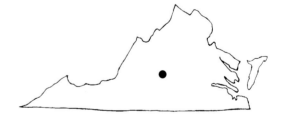

Fares

$95-$185, advance reservations recommended, 50% deposit to confirm, check in 3 p.m., notify if arriving after 6 p.m., out by 11 a.m.

Courtesies

smoke-free environment, children welcome, pet kennel and horse boarding extra

Suzanne Thomas, Suzie Blanchard, Bob Blanchard

Rt 5, Box 460, Locust Dale, VA 22948. 800 385-4936, 540 672-4912 (also FAX). James Madison Highway/Rt 15.

IRIS INN

The crowning glory superlative of this lovely modern home is "a one and only" in Virginia's magnificent offerings of B&Bs — and that is a mural painted by a native daughter who is well on her way to becoming one of the nation's foremost wildlife artists, Joan Henley. Innkeepers Wayne and Iris Karl tapped into brilliance when they commissioned Floyd County born Henley to paint a wildlife scene along the wall of their cathedral common room.

So when you breakfast at Iris Inn, don't be surprised when you feel as though you could simply reach out and touch that doe and her fawn. Every hair, marking, and blade of grass are so vivid you will swear that you are part of that country scene.

Repeat guests will be in for a delightful suprise. Joan Henley has added more of her outstanding wildlife scenes. You will chuckle with laughter at her wit in painting "The Porters" — a scene of two squirrels hoisting a large piece of luggage up the stairs. Her "Hornets' Nest" is a stroke of ingenuity — a real, abandoned hornets' nest installed in a corner 20 feet high and surrounded by painted hornets and a tree branch. Clever, oh so clever.

While many of Virginia's inns are restored old homes, the Iris Inn is different. Your innkeepers built this traditional contemporary on 21 acres of undeveloped oak, dogwood, and chinquapin forest in 1991. Former Midwesterners, the Kansas and Illinois couple left government employment in the Washington, D.C., area to establish this hospitality oasis in Waynesboro.

"We are glad to be living in the woods and welcoming wonderful people each day," they say. Their love of the outdoors is reflected in the wildlife and nature themes of the decor. They paid careful attention to details when they built the home, so guests can be assured of comfort. Each of the seven guest rooms has individually controlled heat and air, pressure balancing showers, and good-sleeping beds!

Your hosts have built a new building with two large, more luxurious units. They come with jacuzzis, showers, gas fireplaces, kitchenettes, balconies, private decks, and exercise equipment. One of the units will convert to a meeting room for 10 people, as the Karls have found half their guests to be business folks (often bringing their spouses, too).

The Iris Inn is too new to have Civil War memories, but your hosts often joke that their inn may be the only B&B in the Valley where Stonewall Jackson did not stay! Their sense of humor may extend to a plaque sometime at the edge of the woods that would read: "We believe Stonewall Jackson camped here."

Hand-painted tiles in the baths and extensive nature prints and original works of art lend colorful notes to the interior. Guests may make themselves at home in the library, great room, hot tub, and tower. The 28-foot rock fireplace in the great room is accented by fieldstone handpicked by Wayne from the Shenandoah Valley. The more than 200 feet of porches allow you to fully enjoy the woodland setting on the western slope of Afton Mountain. Valley views, birds, wildlife, and mountain backdrops abound. Watching the sunset becomes an unparalleled treat.

Wildflower art by Virginia artists earmarks the Wildflower Room, which accommodates guests with a king-size bed, double Jacuzzi, and custom-made furniture. Detached from the main house, Hawks Nest with its cathedral ceiling offers a king-size bed, kitchenette, sitting room, and additional paintings by Virginia artists. Other rooms have queen or king beds and some daybeds.

Juice, fresh fruit, homebaked breads, selected entrees and meats,

coffee, and tea make up your breakfast spread. A bottomless cookie jar resides conveniently in the great room.

Perhaps most of all, the Iris Inn guests enjoy the soft breezes and woodland mountain scenery. The porch rocking chairs ensure that favorite pastime.

In a few short years your innkeepers have established a fine abode for travelers, as attested to by the actions of some recent

guests, who had come to the Iris Inn on business with a leading Waynesboro employer. Before leaving they made weekend reservations to bring their spouses so they, too, could experience the serene ambience.

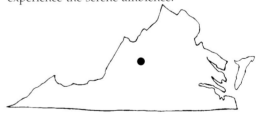

Fares

$75-$95, corporate discounts, 2 night minimum on weekends, deposit of one night or half of stay required, refunded less $10 with 7 day notice, check in 3 p.m. out by 11 a.m.

Courtesies

air conditioning, fans, fireplace, conference facilities for 10, refrigerators, room phone by request, TV in room, handicap access, one unit able to accommodate children, smoking prohibited

Iris and Wayne Karl

191 Chinquapin Dr, Waynesboro VA 22980.
540 943-1991, FAX: 949-4897
From I-64: Exit 96, toward Lyndhurst, then immediate left on Chinquapin Dr, .3 mile to entrance.

JORDAN HOLLOW FARM INN

C radled in the foothills below the Blue Ridge Mountains and across from Massanutten Mountain, Jordan Hollow Farm Inn is party to some of the world's finest outdoor enjoyment and beauty. If you don't mind trekking into the nearby backcountry, you will delight in fly fishing for brook trout in some of the creeks.

There is wilderness to cover in "them thar mountains" so you will want to be careful to take a compass and some U.S. Geological Survey Maps. You are in the heart of the Shenandoah National Park.

New innkeepers have put the restored colonial horse farm high on the rung of wonderful hospitality. Their seasoned staff cooks up some scrumptious meals that will keep you going in your adventure pursuits.

Horses are available at Jordan Hollow to ride around the inn's rolling 150 acres, or guests may arrange to bring their own mounts and stable them. Hundreds of mountain trails abound in the area, with easy access to Shenandoah and the George Washington-Jefferson National Forest. Experienced riders and hikers, both innkeepers can give you firsthand information on where to find the unique areas that are off the beaten path. You might even be able to get Betsy Anderson to guide you to some of her special places of discovery.

Non-equestrians like to walk the inn's trails. Either way, you get to take in the mountain vistas, gorgeous any time of the year, especially from atop the hill behind the inn. The green pastures, trickling streams, and occasional springs around the farm refresh the human spirit.

Across the road from the inn is a park that offers swimming and other recreation activities.

For some guests, the glorious valley and mountain panoramas are what make Jordan Hollow a one-of-a-kind experience. For others, it is the memorable dining to be had at the 200-year-old Farmhouse Restaurant, which features three cozy dining rooms and a small pub. The pub and one of the dining rooms are actually restored log cabins, around which the rest of the house was built. You would be hard pressed to find food any better than the inn's freshly prepared American regional dishes using locally grown produce. For an added touch, the menu includes wines from many Virginia wineries.

There are 21 guest rooms, all with private baths, in two separate lodges. Four of the rooms are in a hand-hewn log building with high ceilings, and they come equipped with fireplaces, whirlpool tubs, cable TV, cozy sitting areas, and private porches. The comfortable rooms afford guests the bonus of a spectacular view of the mountains, meadows, grazing horses, and other farm animals.

All rooms in the wisteria-covered Arbor View Lodge have been redecorated recently with a mingling of interesting antiques and whimsical accent pieces. Each room reflects a different character but all open out to a deck, which of course has the ubiquitous rocker that is just right for reading, relaxing, and simply "porching."

Also recently renovated, the old carriage house sports a comfortable great room. Victorian touches catch your eye when you aren't reading, conversing, playing board games, sipping a glass of sherry, or imagining what the farm was like two centuries ago. Oral history has it that the old farmhouse was used as a Civil War hospital and that close by at Balkymore Hill, Mosby's raiders hid out.

Jordan Hollow dishes out some good, old-fashioned southern hospitality along with a generous dose of serenity. You come here for peace and tranquillity.

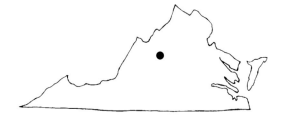

Fares

$100-$140, credit cards accepted, night's deposit required, refunded with 2 day notice, check in 3 p.m., out by noon

Courtesies

air conditioning, private baths, conference facilities, phone in rooms, TV and whirlpool in some rooms, well-behaved children welcome, no pets but horses permitted

Gail Kyle and Betsy Anderson

326 Hawksbill Park Rd, Stanley VA 22851.
540 778-2285, FAX: 778-1759.
From Luray: Rt 340 Business South, go 6 miles left onto Rt 624, left at Rt 689, right at Rt 626.

LIBERTY ROSE

ose Victoria is everyone's favorite guest room at this lushly decorated B&B. The imposing French canopy queen bed embellished with tasseled bed curtains and a luxurious comforter, deep red damask wall covering accented with ivory woodwork, and a tin ceiling dress up these striking quarters.

You can sink in the down-filled sofa and enjoy a movie of your choice from the VCR library, concealed along with the TV in an antique armoire. The large private bath has one of those magnificent clawfooted tubs and a marble shower.

The Suite Williamsburg, just as wonderful as Rose Victoria and furnished with equally outstanding antiques, offers the utmost of privacy and is ideally suited for honeymooners. All four rooms at this Williamsburg inn have plush but firm quality mattresses, which guarantee you a great night's sleep, and the most sumptuous bathrooms you will ever find.

Amenities run the gamut: cushy bathrobes, bubble bath for the porcelain clawfooted tubs, a bowl full of chocolates in each room, and always, a silk rose for the lady.

The detail in decorating is so original and interesting that, after staying at Liberty Rose, guests have been known to comment, "It makes us want to go home and redecorate our house!" But your innkeepers are what complete the B&B experience: Brad and Sandi Hirz, a really fun couple that make you feel as though their house is yours.

Brad, a young retired farmer, is the breakfast chef. Interior designer Sandi has crafted the handiwork so artfully displayed throughout the 1920s home. She executed all the bed coverings, drapery treatments, wall coverings, and other special touches, and does not hesitate to share all the tricks of the trade with inquiring guests.

Sandi's eclectic mix incorporates English, Victorian, French country, and 18th century antiques, wallpapers, and fabrics — appealing to home lovers of all kinds.

Not only does each day bring a different breakfast, but sometimes the venue becomes the outdoor courtyard. After coffee and juice, the main course might be scrambled eggs and crisp bacon with stuffed French toast and fresh fruit. You are welcome to open any time a well-stocked "fridge" of complimentary soft drinks and munch on Brad's famous chocolate chip cookies.

Good books and a roaring fire provide for some quiet moments, or you may opt to entertain yourself playing the grand piano.

If you are an outdoor aficionado, you will enjoy the heavily wooded hill on which the house is located; a natural relaxed setting boasts century-old beech, oak, and poplar trees.

Built by a prominent family nearly 70 years ago, Liberty Rose sits on one of the few hills in the relatively flat town of Williamsburg along a historical corridor, the road to Jamestown. It is one mile from the College of William and Mary and Merchant Square of Colonial Williamsburg juncture.

The two-storied, white clapboard house has a dormered slate roof, flanked by twin chimneys. Much of the brick used was "picked up" at Jamestown. All the rooms have window views on three sides to create a feeling of environmental closeness.

There is no place like home, and here you feel you have stumbled upon one that evokes the same intimate feelings. And even if you may not be the world's greatest feline lover, you will fall for Mister Goose, the 22-pound outdoor kitty who greets, welcomes, and is

always at the drive to bid farewell and beg guests to return.

Your innkeepers, who fell in love with each other and this house in 1986, were married and affectionately refer to Liberty Rose as Williamsburg's most romantic B&B. The then-empty old house was their honeymoon project! And that's why Sandi and Brad say they are making their own legends...

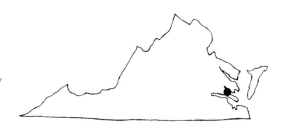

Fares

$120-$225, full prepayment required within 7 days of booking, night's deposit refunded with 18 day notice, check in 3 p.m., out by 11 a.m.

Courtesies

shuttle from train station, air conditioning, private baths, 2 fireplaces, refrigerator use, phones, TVs/VCRs and movies in all rooms, children over 12 welcome, no smoking allowed inside

Brad and Sandi Hirz

1022 Jamestown Rd, Williamsburg VA 23185. 800 545-1825, 757 253-1260.

LLEWELLYN LODGE AT LEXINGTON

omfort, comfort, and more comfort are what you will find at this in-town inn, which at one time operated as a tourist home. Your hosts, who opened their doors to travelers in 1985, also have an extensive background that qualifies them well as innkeepers.

For more than 30 years Ellen Roberts has worked in the airline, travel, hotel, and restaurant arenas. When she moved to Lexington she met John Roberts, a local. He lent her a hacksaw blade, then married her!

While your yummy breakfasts will come from gourmet cook Ellen, revelations concerning the region's best fishing holes are via John. He's a veritable treasure trove of visitor information and has extensive maps and computer trail guides for both hiking and cycling. If you twist his arm, he might take you fly fishing.

The 58-year-old brick colonial home rests in the old residential part of Lexington near the historic district. It's within a convenient walk to the home of Stonewall Jackson; Washington and Lee University and its Robert E. Lee Chapel — a Civil War buff's must; Virginia Military Institute and its Marshall Museum; and other fascinating sites.

Llewellyn Lodge's good value and terrific breakfast bring many a repeat visitor and referral. Ellen whips up a queen's omelet, Belgian waffles with pure Virginia maple syrup, bacon, ham, sausage, homemade breads, and muffins. To keep you charged during the day, she provides iced tea spiced with mint from the garden, sodas, cookies, and peanuts. In the winter months, you can sip her hot cider or tea by the fireplace to warm up the innards.

Ellen and John are continually adding refinements to their pleasant abode. All six bedrooms have extra firm beds, ceiling fans, and personal bathrooms. A Shaker pencil post queen bed captures the focal point of one room, whose bath has a tub and shower. Wicker furniture, a queen bed, and stall shower make up a second room. An oak spindle queen bed, easy chair, and stall shower mark a third upstairs room.

Room four has a king bed, sitting area, TV, and tub/shower combination. A fifth room features two brass double beds and a stall shower and is conducive for family stays. The final room, located on the first floor to accommodate handicapped persons who do not need a wheelchair, has a twin set of four-poster beds and a tub/shower.

In addition to Lexington's immediate attractions, there are abundant things to see and do in the neighboring vicinity. The Lime Kiln Arts Center, which enjoys a growing reputation, presents regional historical dramas and concerts in an outdoor setting.

You can hike on the Chessie Trail (a seven-mile walking trail from Lexington to Buena Vista along an old railroad bed beside the Maury River), bicycle over back country roads, canoe down the Maury River, tube and picnic at Goshen Pass, trout fish the glorious waters flowing out of the mountains into the valleys, peruse the antique shops, golf, play tennis, or view equestrian events at the impressive Virginia Horse Center.

After a full day, it's easy to unwind out on Llewellyn's deck or relax by the fire with a good book or lively conversation in the living room. You could also head for the TV room if you wanted to pursue that American pastime. Lexington's array of fine restaurants more than satisfies any dining needs. And the friendly atmosphere at Llewellyn is most winsome.

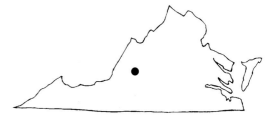

Fares

$65+, discount for seniors, government and corporate discount, a night's deposit or credit card guarantee, refunded with 1 day notice, check in 2-7 p.m., out by 11 a.m.

Courtesies

central air conditioning, private baths, refrigerator use, washer and dryer access, limited handicap access, children over 10 years welcome, no pets, smoking restricted

Ellen and John Roberts

603 South Main St, Lexington, VA 24450.
800 882-1145, 540 463-3235, FAX: 464-3122
Email Lll603@aol.com
From I-81: Exit at Rt. 11 into Lexington, go approximately 4 miles.

LYNCHBURG
MANSION INN

eading up the parade of federal and Victorian mansions on a street still paved in turn-of-the-century brick, this imposing 9,000-square-foot Spanish Georgian mansion was built in 1914 for self-made millionaire James R. Gilliam at a then princely cost of $86,000. Mr. Gilliam had by far the highest income in the Hill City.

The Lynchburg Mansion Inn Bed and Breakfast sits on a half acre in the Garland Hill Historic District, which is on the National Register of Historic Places. The inn has been on the garden tours during Historic Garden Week in Virginia.

During part of the 1800s, Lynchburg was the second wealthiest city in America. The city's great tobacco and iron days made possible the creation of an unusually large number of mansions and lovely gardens.

The city is also loaded with Civil War lore. Fort Early served as the city's outer defense in 1864 against attack by Union General Hunter, who headquartered at Sandusky. Lynchburg's Old City Cemetery has a Civil War section, and Spring Hill Cemetery is another resting place for many confederates. Riverside Park contains a locally-built boat used to haul the wounded during the Civil War; along the James River are factories that served as hospitals. The Pest House Medical Museum is a monument to those who died of smallpox during the war. The city is the birthplace of Douglas S. Freeman, Washington and Lee biographer. Appomattox, the final destination of Lee's retreat and thus where the Civil War ended, is a half-hour away.

Lynchburg Mansion Inn epitomizes beauty, elegance, and fine workmanship. Inside are unequaled cherry and oak woodwork, the lavish patterns of fine fabrics, rooms full of mahogany, gleaming crystal and brass, gold-embellished service plates, antique silver, three solariums, original central vacuum, an unusually large number of original bathrooms, and the ultimate in guest amenities.

Outside are gardens of flowering plum and cherry trees, ornamental and specimen plantings, palms, and bright annuals spilling from giant clay pots. Monumental porticoes highlight the 105-foot wraparound veranda. A six-foot-high iron fence surrounds the mansion and its carriage house.

Immense Ionic columns ring the mansion's porte-cochere, the demi-lunar side portico, and the entry portico. Double doors open onto the 50-foot grand hall with soaring ceilings, wide cherry columns, and a grand staircase that winds up three stories.

Architect Stanhope Johnson presciently designed the house so that windows would be shielded from strong sun, gardens would receive the southern sun, and side porticoes and exterior doors would catch the east-west breezes.

Owners/innkeepers Bob and Mauranna Sherman restored this wonderful old home to its former glory with 15 to 20 workmen on site daily for six months.

Bedrooms with private ensuite bathrooms, cable TV, phone, luxurious linens, double-thick towels, fragrant sprays, sweet soaps, extra feather pillows, and Persian and Aubusson design rugs make you more than comfortable!

Business travelers will find the desks in their rooms handy. An outdoor spa bubbles with massaging jets, while a cozy place to escape inside is the well stocked library.

The Veranda Suite, decorated in hunter and garnet, paisley, plaid, and foulard, encompasses the original master bedroom and private, light-filled solarium. Lush pillows on the high king bed rest against the seven-foot headboard.

The solarium features a tapestry sleep sofa, delightful table and chairs, microwave for popcorn, and a refrigerator stocked with sodas.

The Garden Suite's private entrance opens onto the gardens. Ralph Lauren linens adorn the bedroom of the apartment-sized accommodations.

A four-poster, rice-carved mahogany king bed with steps and Persian style rugs compose the Gilliam Room. Laura Ashley linens and fabrics and Battenburg lace enhance the country French Bowen Room. Blue and white Waverly fabrics, nostalgic wicker, seashells from around the world, and an antique steamer trunk characterize the crisp and airy Nantucket Room.

You wake up to coffee and juice on a silver tray, along with a newspaper, set near your room. A complete breakfast, which varies from day to day, is served in the formal dining room in high style. One morning you might sample a first course of raspberry pears, then peach French toast and center-cut bacon decorated with pansies, bachelor's buttons, and an

enormous nasturtium leaf.

The Shermans, who hold a deep commitment to their Christian faith, maintain an abiding interest in historic properties, art, music, books, and landscaping. Bob who owned a real estate business in Alexandria, is a broker with Century 21 in Lynchburg. Mauranna enjoys writing and painting and is currently working on ink and watercolor portrayals of the mansions of Lynchburg.

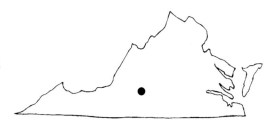

Fares

$84+, business discount, night's deposit required, refunded with 10 day notice except May and October, check in 3-6 p.m.

Courtesies

air conditioning, private baths, fireplaces, conference and wedding facilities, refrigerator use, phone and TV in room, washer/dryer use, smoking only on the veranda

Bob and Mauranna Sherman

*405 Madison, Lynchburg VA 24504.
Reservations: 800 352-1199, 804 528-5400.
From Rt 29 Business, which also becomes 5th St, going S turn right onto Madison St, inn on left.*

MANOR AT TAYLOR'S STORE

hen you enter between the massive brick columns with granite plaques announcing "Taylor's Store, Circa 1799" and drive alongside the 200-year-old chestnut split-rail fence, you immediately sense the historical nature that hallmarks the Manor at Taylor's Store. The secluded 120-acre estate in the foothills of the Blue Ridge Mountains at Smith Mountain Lake offers a true getaway for relaxation, recreation, and romance.

Taylor's Store, the state historical marker in front of the home informs you, was a trading post founded on this site in 1799 by Skelton Taylor, a 1st Lieutenant in Virginia's Bedford Militia. It served as an ordinary, U.S. Post Office, and the hub of the community during its day as a 19th century rural frontier. The adjacent corn field was used as a "muster field" during the Civil War.

The manor house was originally constructed in 1820 by John D. Booth and was the focus of a prosperous tobacco plantation.

A fire in the 1890s destroyed much of the brick home, which was immediately rebuilt on the original brick foundation using hand tools cut off the plantation. Lt. Moses L. Booth, 2nd Virginia Calvalry, was killed in battle in 1861 and his grave in the family cemetery is marked with the Southern Cross. Nearly a hundred years and much renovation later, Lee and Mary Lynn Tucker transformed the manor into a first class B&B inn.

Private porches, fireplace's, luxurious baths, and splendid views are just a few of the special features found in the nine guest rooms at the inn.

Christmas Cottage, a separate three-bedroom/two-bath accommodation, is perfect for families with children or guest desiring complete privacy. This comfortably furnished cabin offers a fully equipped kitchen, den with fireplace, and a large deck with views of the ponds and surronding wilderness

Guests at the manor are treated to a full, "heart healthy" gourmet breakfast, served in the dining room with gorgeous views and crowded birdfeeders as morning entertainment. The crepes, pancakes, waffles, French toast, and other house specialties are featured in Mary Lynn's nationally acclaimed cookbook, "Heart Healthy Hospitality." Homemade breads, fresh fruits, and freshly ground coffee get the day off to a great start.

Infinite opportunities for activities, both inside and outside, are available at the Manor at Taylor's Store. There are a billiard room, exercise room, guest kitchen, library, large screen TV with movies, great room with games and fireplace, formal parlor with grand piano, and sun room with panoramic views of the countryside. The hot tub, on an enclosed lattice porch, is a favorite spot for relaxing.

Six private, spring-fed ponds on the estate invite swimming, fishing, and canoeing. Nearby, Smith Mountain Lake provides additional recreational apportunities, as does the Blue Ridge Parkway, only 20 minutes away.

Your innkeepers, Lee and Mary Lynn Tucker, engage in a variety of interests, avocations, and involvements. Lee, a pathologist, is also a vintner and wine enthusiast, sailor, musician, historian, and an expert renovator of old buildings.

Mary Lynn, a former nurse practitioner with expertise in nutrition, manages the B&B , was founding president of the Bed and Breakfast Association of Virginia, and spends spare moments caring for her horse and dog, writing, sailing, playing music, and enjoying life in the country. The Tuckers' easygoing form of hospitality sets guests at ease and invites you to make yourself at home at the Manor at Taylor's Store bed and breakfast inn.

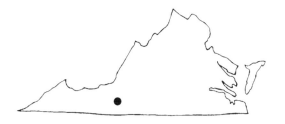

Fares

$85-$185, night's deposit required, refunded with week notice, check in 4-6 p.m. (flexible), out by 11 a.m.

Courtesies

central air conditioning, conference facilities, children welcome in cottage, no smoking in the manor house but permitted in cottage, picnic lunches and European dinner baskets available, gift baskets for special occasions, ABC license, catering for events on and off site.

Mary Lynn and Lee Tucker

Rt 1, Box 533, Smith Mountain Lake VA 24184. 800 772-9984, 540 721-3951, FAX: 721-5243 On Rt. 122, 1.6 miles north of Burnt Chimney intersection at Rt 116, 3.7 miles south of Booker T. Washington National Monument.

MEADOW
LANE LODGE

utdoor enthusiasts feel as though they have landed in paradise after weaving along the country backroads through the meadows and woods to get here. When so much of the East has been swallowed up in development, it's incredible to behold a true wilderness and nature preserve area.

And the good news at Meadow Lane Lodge is that its pristine environment keeps staying pure! In fact, the owners' sensitivity to the natural resources has recently received the highest tribute imaginable — bald eagles are now soaring the magnificent heights that loom beyond the valley floor.

Helping to protect the virgin, 1,600-acre estate is the surrounding George Washington National Forest. To further ensure that the oasis remains intact, the owners have obtained an open space easement for the farm through the Virginia Outdoors Foundation so that it remains an unspoiled place of beauty in perpetuity. And for those guests who want to be directly in touch with nature, Meadow Lane Lodge can provide fully outfitted camping for a night along the Jackson River.

Hiking trails, all 20 miles of them, are marked to prevent the uninitiated from getting lost, and every season harbors a specialness. In spring you forage through thickets of redbud, dogwood, and early blooming wildflowers. Summer gives way to rhododendron, mountain laurel, and chirping song birds. Fall foliage in the Allegheny mountains casts a colorful bouquet beyond compare. And even winter yields its own beauty when the leaves are off the deciduous trees and you can more fully see the contours of the ridges and land formations.

Fly fishermen quietly claim their sport doesn't get any better than here, especially in the spring. Owners Philip and Catherine Hirsh and innkeepers Steve and Cheryl Hooley yearly stock the sparkling Jackson

River that flows through the property with brown and rainbow trout. The lodge is the home of the renowned Orvis Fly Fishing School in May.

The crystal clear waters, running for two miles on the property, are also home to small mouth bass, rock bass, blue gills, pickerel, and fall fish. Catch and release is the rule. Canoeing and swimming are other favorite pastimes at Meadow Lane.

Wildlife watchers will thrill at "The Deck," one of the most marvelous observatories in the state. The railed, wooden platform overlooks a beaver slough, the Jackson River valley, and all manner of life that comes to feed and drink — deer, fox, blue heron, a spectrum of birds, including the rare bald eagle. If it's indigenous to Virginia, you will find the flora and fauna in this quiet corner of the state.

The lodge's main barns, dating from the 1920s when Meadow Lane was a horse breeding farm, are full of friendly domestic animals. You may wake to the sound of roosters. A Guernsey cow, horse, donkey, sheep, and peacocks roam freely with their companions, the resident geese, chickens, and ducks.

Owned by the Hirsh family for three generations, Meadow Lane traces its earliest history back to an original land grant from King George III of England to Charles Lewis, one of Virginia's prominent early settlers.

The foundation of an old log cabin, circa 1750, is visible from the early 19th century slave cabin on the west side of the Jackson River. A stockade was built around the cabin during the French and Indian War and eventually became known as Fort Dinwiddie. George Washington is said to have visited the fort twice in 1755.

Present structures date from the early 1800s to the 1960s. The lodge, as well kept as its manicured croquet course, is simply but tastefully decorated. Two imposing stone fireplaces set off the gracious living room. There is some air conditioning, but in this cool mountain setting you are seldom uncomfortable.

You can choose from among 14 spotless and wonderfully comfortable rooms. The Bay Window Room in Craig's Cottage, so named because it provides a wide angle view of the farm and meadows, features a king-size bed, private bath, and fireplace, which adds to its romantic aura.

The Car Barn is ideal for two couples or a small family with its two rooms and baths. A living room is loaded with lots of windows. The front porch looks out on the meadow where the menagerie of farm animals roam.

The lodge's newest addition is the Granary, a 100-year-old restored grain barn cottage. This magnificent structure, overlooking the Jackson River, sports three bedrooms, full kitchen, dining room, great room, a pair of porches, and a breathtaking view.

Your hosts take breakfast very seriously — not only will you come away from the table filled, but supremely satisfied. Cooked with a southern influence, the popular dishes include cream chicken over waffles, batterbread, roast beef hash, and popovers. From April to October, the lodge offers dinner to guests on Fridays and Saturdays and will prepare picnic lunches upon request.

You can come here to enjoy the outdoors at its best, or just linger in a state of repose. If you want to scout the regional landmarks, there are nearby points of interest: the Bacova Guild showroom of nationally acclaimed items made in local Bath County; the Garth Newel Music Center of growing repute; Cascades golf course at the famed Homestead Resort; and the next valley over to Snowshoe, the best skiing in the South. Or, you can "take the waters" at the Warm Springs pools.

Meadow Lane Lodge enjoys a steady repeat business, so you will want to book holiday weekends far in advance.

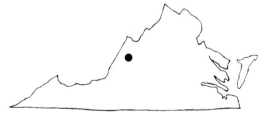

Fares

$115+, night's deposit required, refunded with 10 day notice, check in 2 p.m., out by noon

Courtesies

private baths, several fireplaces, screened porches, conference facilities for 18, phone and TV in some rooms, laundry service available, limited handicap access, children welcome, smoke-free environment

Philip and Catherine Hirsh, Owners
Steve and Cheryl Hooley, Innkeepers

Route 1, Box 110, Warm Springs VA 24484.
540 839-5959, FAX: 839-2135.
4 1/2 miles west of Rt 220 on Rt 39.

MIDDLEBURG
COUNTRY INN

icture-perfect towns, unsurpassed scenery, hospitable folks, and
rich heritage mark the Virginia landscape, almost like no other state
in America. These definitions all reside in one of the nation's most
quaint little places, Middleburg, in the heart of the Commonwealth's
horse country.

The hunt country jewel is beautifully restored and carefully preserved
by loving residents. It also entices any shopper with a fascinating array of
designer boutiques, jewelry shops, antique dealers, and art galleries.

Called "Middleburg" because it was midway between Alexandria and
Winchester, the tiny town appeared on colonial Virginia maps as early as
1731 and was then known as Chinn's Crossroads. The population has
remained more or less the same and today only numbers 550.

Originally surveyed by George Washington, Middleburg was
alternately held by the Union and the Confederacy during the
Civil War.

To enjoy the 18th century community to the hilt, you will discover
Middleburg Country Inn right off Washington Street, where the old-
fashioned horse buggy is parked. Ample parking for guests is a plus
because you can easily walk anywhere around town.

For a century and a half, the Middleburg Country Inn served as the
Episcopal rectory of this hunt country. Originally, Abner Gibson
purchased the lots from the town's founder, Leven Powell, for $141.52.
Gibson, a lawyer and manufacturer of wagons and wagon wheels, was
one of 21 heads of families listed in the 1810 census. Early in 1856, Johns
Parish vestrymen purchased for $1,200 the lots with the brick dwelling,
which then saw use as a parsonage. The parish owned the home until
1987, when it was sold to the current owner who opened it as an inn in
1990.

A three-story red brick building, the inn offers six guest rooms with private baths. Each room is furnished in the colonial period and has a fireplace. You sleep in four-poster canopied beds, as did your forefathers. Furnishings include cable TV and VCR.

The interiors bask in the romantic 18th century elegance with luxurious appointments and rich, burgundy colors abounding. While you can snuggle up to a cozy fire, your 20th century delights reside in such amenities as the bubbling heated hot tub on the terrace. Robes are furnished to guests to wear outside.

On weekends and holidays, the candlelight gourmet dinners that come with lodging, highlighted by a five-course chef's choice, are a memorable treat. Guests savor the full country breakfast, which also takes place in the Lafayette Dining Room. You feast on fruits, old style waffles, breads and cakes, eggs a la English muffins and bacon, eggs Benedict, jellies, cereals, and Sumatra Mandheling coffee.

Nearby are a health club and horseback riding. Of course, you can spend days in the nation's capital. Piedmont and Meredyth vineyards are area jaunts. As Capital of Virginia's Hunt Country, Middleburg positions you at the starting gate for its popular spring and fall steeplechase and point to point races.

Long a home to those who loved horses, Middleburg started Virginia's first foxhunt. Richard Henry Dulaney established the tradition in 1840. Today the surrounding countryside is an unspoiled, immaculately kept farming area of gently rolling terrains with beautiful stately homes of the 1800s. The countryside is groomed as smartly as any golf course.

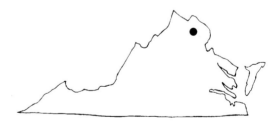

Fares

weekday: $95-$145 (includes breakfast), weekend and holiday: $165-215 for king or queen bedrooms (includes breakfast and dinner), $225-$295 for bridal suites with Jacuzzi, special commercial and conference rates, deposit, refunded with 7 day notice, check in 2 p.m., out by 11 a.m.

Courtesies

air conditioning, working fireplaces, cable TV, in-room videos and phone, smoking on terrace, conference facilities, handicap access, Dulles International Airport close by

Susan and John Pettibone

P.O. Box 2065
209 E. Washington St, Middleburg VA 22117.
800 262-6082, 540 687-6082, FAX: 687-5603.
40 miles west from Washington, D.C., on Rt 50 W.

NORTH BEND PLANTATION

are is the occasion when you can stay at a historic property owned and managed by its descendants! Just as rare runs the testimony from your hosts that "we've been a B&B for eleven years, have never had a complaint, and we've loved being innkeepers."

North Bend Plantation, in the deep country of rural Charles City County, was built in 1819 using designs of the leading builder-architect of his time, Asher Benjamin. It was the home of Sarah Harrison, sister of William Henry Harrison, who was the ninth president of the United States. During the Civil War, General Sheridan used the home as his headquarters. Today the original outbuildings and Greek revival style home are on the National Historic Register and Virginia Historic Landmark listing.

The handsome, two-story frame home showcases the federal period with its original mantles, staircase carvings, and original woodgraining on the pocket doors. Surrounded by 850 acres of land remaining under cultivation by the owners, the plantation home contains antiques original to the house and family. High rooms, beautifully appointed with views of magnificent vistas, include a library of old and rare books as well as Mathew Brady's Civil War photographs.

There is a fireplace in every room. The 6,000-square-foot home features rooms that average 20-feet-square. Four bedrooms, decorated with Laura Ashley designs and furnished with extra-firm, custom-made mattresses, are open to guests. Just off the upstairs sun porch, the Rose Room comes with a private bath and reading area. You sleep in a queen canopy bed with an unusual antique armoire nearby. The large seven-by-seven-foot furnishing is made of solid mahogany and has a diamond-dust mirror.

Another solid mahogany piece, a tester bed dating 1810, resides in the Sheridan Room, named after General Sheridan, who used North Bend as his headquarters in 1864 while his corps built the pontoon bridge over the James River in preparation for the devastating Battle of Petersburg. The bed belonged to Edmund Ruffin, the illustrious Southerner who fired "the shot heard round the world" to begin the Civil War. History's ironic fate is that the bed's headboard was shot out during the war.

The other conversational piece in this room is General Sheridan's desk, where later were found the maps of his breastworks (Civil War trenches). He had 30,000 union troops parked in the area. Today you can still view the breastworks around the eastern edge of the plantation country home.

According to oral history, General Sheridan had a temper fit here and stuck his sword in one of the panel doors, splitting it. In its more genteel times, the home played host to numerous parties. One frequent guest was President Tyler and his second wife, Julia Gardiner, 30 years his junior and one of the nation's most flamboyant First Ladies. The hospitality that Julia loved at North Bend continues this day and has been written up in *Country Home Magazine*, the *New York Times*, the *Washington Post*, and *Southern Living*.

George and Ridgely Copland are the plantation's hospitable hosts. The great great grandson of Edmund Ruffin, George is also the great great nephew of President Harrison. His mother was a Ruffin of Evelynton Plantation, and his maternal grandmother a Harrison of Berkeley Plantation.

You will find enjoyment in the billiards room and on the three inviting porches, where you can scan the horizons of fields planted with corn and beans. On any one day you are liable to see deer grazing the fields and wild ducks and geese flying overhead. Some days you may catch a glimpse of

the Princess Ann Hunt Club fox hunting across the land.

A walloping breakfast in the dining room packs in bacon, sausage, homemade waffles, juice, seasonal cantaloupe, honeydew melons, and strawberries. If your visit comes during the summer months, lemonade beside the pool refreshes you after arrival.

Besides swimming you can go on nature walks around the plantation, play croquet, enjoy the tandem bike, pitch some horseshoes, play a friendly volleyball game, or hit some birdies in badminton. You are a 30-minute ride from Colonial

Williamsburg, the famous Petersburg Battlefields, and Richmond's Confederate Museum.

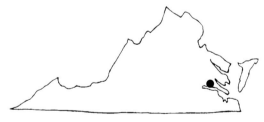

Fares

$105-$135, discounts to airlines, travel agents, military; deposit required, refunded with 2 week notice except on holidays, check in 3 p.m., out by 11 a.m.

Courtesies

air conditioning, ceiling fans, private baths, refrigerator use, children 6 and over welcome, smoking restricted

George and Ridgely Copland

12200 Weyanoke Rd, Charles City VA 23030. 800 841-1479, 804 829-5176. Just off Historic Rt 5 on Weyanoke Rd.

OAKS
VICTORIAN INN

hy else would this one of a kind, picture-perfect home be named The Oaks except for its gigantic, towering oaks believed to be more than 300 years old. There are seven champion trees, one of which may be nearly 400 years old and is documented as one of the largest white oaks in the Commonwealth.

It's very possible there is no setting in America more majestic. The hilltop Queen Anne Victorian in Southwest Virginia embodies the romantic image idealized in novels. Leave it to an architect and a former public relations executive to find this pearl and realize its potential for a bed and breakfast inn. Tom and Margaret Ray purchased the outstanding house in 1989 and converted it into a country inn catering to the leisure and business traveler.

Floor to ceiling windows allow the outside light to flood the interiors so that even on overcast days the house is radiant. Turrets create interesting exteriors and interiors. Stained-glass windows remind you this is a home of yesteryear, while a beautiful two-level oak staircase reigns as the focal point in the reception hall.

A large wraparound porch is what makes the exterior so inviting. Guests also enjoy the backyard terrace with its perennial gardens and fish pond, and are not hard pressed to find a comfortable niche in which to have morning coffee, read the newspaper, or watch the birds feeding.

You will find every amenity that differentiates bed and breakfasts from standard lodging. Soft, luxurious linens, the ultimate in comfortable mattresses, spacious common areas that give you the feeling of home, personal attention. Two parlors with interesting fireplaces occupy the first floor and provide the ample common space.

Decorating is geared toward comfortable elegance. Most of the furniture and accessories belong to your hosts and include gifts, heirlooms, and a mix of antiques. Margaret loves fabric and has made the most of the fashionable window treatments, pillows, and bedskirts. Some of the bedcovers are extremely old, treasures acquired over the years. Antique linens accent the decors.

Five guest rooms provide bedding quarters. There are his and hers bathrooms in the Bonnie Victoria Room. "Hers" has a 102-year-old clawfoot bathtub that is original to the house. You can snooze in the king canopy bed beside the charm of a gas log fireplace and decorating touches of oriental rugs, wing chairs, crocheted lace, and chintz.

The Julia Pierce Room in the second floor turret with five large windows offers views of spectacular sunsets and is named after the woman who give birth to seven babies here. A handpainted slate fireplace with gas logs lends warm elegance to the room decorated in peaches and cream. The large bathroom has a dressing area that brings relaxing pleasure with its jacuzzi for two. Honeymooners love this suite.

Three-course breakfasts in the formal dining room receive rave reviews. Served by candlelight with Dresden china, sterling silver, lace tablecloths, linen napkins, and classical music, all food is prepared that morning from gourmet recipes in the New Orleans, Charleston, and old Virginia traditions. Special consideration is given to low cholesterol cooking.

Complimentary sherry, sodas, tea, and coffee are always available. Additional treats include fresh cookies, homemade ice cream, fresh fruit, and assorted nibbles.

Guests may peruse The Oaks' extensive library of books and

magazines, view some old movies via the VCR, play chess, checkers, and other games, or go for a warming soak in the hot tub under the garden gazebo.

The Rays' beloved pets act as The Oaks' social directors — Wonder Dog Lulu, a Scottish terrier; and a feisty West Highland terrier named Ms. Kaile Bonnie Faire. This cast of characters quickly endears themselves to guests and often receives a trail of letters.

Located in the historic section atop Christiansburg's highest hill, the imposing home was built in 1889 as a wedding gift for Mrs. Pierce. Major W.L. Pierce, a real estate investor, was beloved in this small community and is remembered as a man who taught his daughter and chums to dance in the attic playroom. Remaining in the family until 1982 and named to the National Register of Historic Places in 1993, The Oaks is situated on one and a half acres of beautifully landscaped lawn amid a quiet residential neighborhood. The inn is convenient to both Virginia Tech and Radford University.

Every December the inn

celebrates a Victorian Christmas all decked out in appropriate finery. Several 10-foot Christmas trees from a nearby tree plantation are decorated with Victorian ornaments — a growing tradition, with entertainment provided by area musicians.

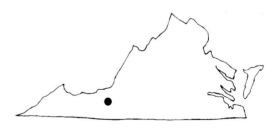

Fares

$100+, corporate rates Sun-Thurs, 2.5% surcharge with credit card payments, check in 4-8 p.m. (please advise if later arrival), out by noon

Courtesies

shuttle transportation for added cost, bedrooms air conditioned and with ceiling fans, all private baths, 8 fireplaces, sunroom available for meetings of 20, all bedrooms have cable TV and a small refrigerator, phone in rooms, children over 14 welcome, good kennel nearby, smoking permitted outside

Margaret and Tom Ray

311 East Main St, Christiansburg VA 24073.
540 381-1500.
Internet: http://www.travelassist.com/reg/vall71.html
or http://www.specialplaces.com/va/oaks.htm
From I-81: Exit 114, follow Main St into town 2 miles, bear right at Park St, then left into driveway.

PALMER
COUNTRY
MANOR

There is just no end to the surprises you will come upon in the Virginia countryside. If you accidentally find your vehicle turning into Palmer Country Manor, then you must be living right. Your best bet is to carve out a date and make it a point to get there.

While Palmer lies in the rolling piedmont, only 15 minutes from Monticello and 45 minutes from the Charlottesville airport, the neatly trimmed 1830 estate now encompasses 180 secluded acres. It is an easily accessible wilderness.

The vacation paradise relaxes patrons with its ten private cottages. Each comes with an expansive living area endowed with a fireplace, color TV, four poster country pine bed, handcarved armoire, private bath, and an ample deck that views an inviting forest and lush meadows.

Bedrooms are all lovingly and gracefully furnished to reflect some history of the plantation and surrounding region. Beds are queen or king. And there are some Jacuzzi tubs around!

Your smorgasbord of fine accommodations also include the option of staying in the historic plantation house. The manor is one of the few B&Bs conducive for families; its rooms can sleep up to four people. Day care for children is also available.

The restored old house has a library, comfortable parlor, and screened porch that is always a hit.

The varied menu of activities means there is something for everyone in the family: 18-hole golf at a nearby country club, swimming in the on-site pool, fishing in the manor's spring-fed pond, hiking through the woods and fields, romanticizing with champagne in a hot air balloon, white water rafting on the James, wine tasting at one of the 14 local vineyards and at the inn on selected weekends, and fine dining.

You have access to horseback riding or you can grab a tube and float down the Rivanna River. Sightseers never tire of Monticello, where the gardens are the most recent restoration effort; Ash Lawn; Michie Tavern; or University of Virginia.

Your hosts provide a trail map of the property so you can successfully navigate the path of your choice. McCary's Trail, named after the first owner of the plantation, winds one mile through the woods behind the cottages. The Deer Path starts at the metal barn and meanders through the fields and woods to a picnic area, then follows the creek to turn at a small ravine. It continues on an old logging road back to the start.

Lanford Run, named after the family that owned the plantation for the longest duration, takes you around a mile loop and is perfect for joggers. Some guests like to bring their bikes and explore the quiet country roads. No city congestion with which to contend!

The original property took in 2,500 acres and was called Solitude. It changed hands through the years and was opened July 14, 1989, as Palmer Country Manor.

A rousing breakfast starts your day. An additional pleasure is a five-course candlelight dinner each night if you opt for the Modified American Plan.

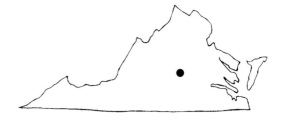

Fares

$75-$155 (varies with season and if MAP), credit cards or checks for deposits, confirm with 1 night deposit, refunded with 48 hour notice, 2 night stay required holiday and special college weekends

Courtesies

air conditioning, fireplaces, private baths, Jacuzzi, swimming pool, hiking trails, children welcome

Kathy and Greg Palmer

Rt. 2, Box 1390, Palmyra VA 22963.
800 253-4306, FAX: 804 589-1300.
20 miles SE of Charlottesville on Rt 640 (off Rt 15).

PINEY GROVE
AT SOUTHALL'S
PLANTATION

Thousands of acres of wildlife along the Chickahominy River bid you welcome to this secluded country retreat. While the peace and tranquility may cause you to think you are far afield from civilization, you are actually convenient to Williamsburg.

Located in a remote area of Charles City County among the famed James River plantations, Piney Grove has been meticulously restored and epitomizes exactly what B&B travelers desire — history, elegant accommodations, gracious hospitality, the old effortlessly combined with modern conveniences.

Twenty miles west of Williamsburg, Charles City County is as rural as rural gets. In fact, a barnyard of farm animals will greet you at Piney Grove — chickens, ducks, geese, ponies, sheep, goats, and rabbits.

Working farms surround this Virginia Historic Landmark and National Register of Historic Places property, once home to the Chickahominy Indians. Charles City Sheriff Furnea Southall established the prosperous 300-acre plantation, later owned during the Civil War by Edmund A. Saunders, a successful Richmond wholesale grocer who contributed to the Confederacy's Commissary, and then Thomas Fletcher Harwood, who lost a leg in the Battle of Malvern Hill. Harwood re-enlisted and was later captured at Gettysburg. He returned to Piney Grove, enlarged the house, and is buried on the property.

In the dining room hang several Civil War maps that picture Piney Grove. The parlor contains depictions of Malvern Hill and supply depots at Berkeley Plantation, where McClellan headquartered. Guests are free to delve into the volumes of Civil War history there.

A Chickahominy Indian site, unmarked slave graves, the Harwood family cemetery, and the springs that form the headwaters of Rippons Run are noteworthy. Piney Grove itself is a rare survival of the

Virginia Tidewater log building. The Ladysmith plantation residence reflects the modest Greek revival style. To get their B&B up and running, the owners undertook a multi-year restoration program of the log structure (circa 1800, Tidewater Virginia's oldest and best preserved example), Ladysmith, Ashland and Duck Church.

The restored elegance of bygone days lives after all their hard work. You will find fresh flowers, spacious rooms with high ceilings, sterling silver, pewterware, down comforters, roaring fires in the log room, brandy in the parlor-library, a mint julep on the gazebo, and good hearts to meet your every need and make your visit memorable. The Gordineers lovingly share their home and the heritage of the James River Plantation Country. Brian is the resident historian with expertise in architectural history.

Five immaculate bedrooms serve the traveler. The rising sun illumines the stained-glass window in the Richard Boulware Room and gently reminds you it's morning. At night you can relax in the wing chair by a fire and watch the sunset over the pony pasture or the birds swooping around the gardens. Unique to this room are the 1859 "wheat sheaves and stars" stenciling design, and farm scenes from *Harpers Weekly* and *Leslie's Illustrated.*

Your full breakfast stands you in good stead during the day. Ample portions of fresh fruit and juice, Virginia ham, Piney Grove's own farm-fresh eggs, and homemade bread are set on the table in the log room by an open fire in the cooler months. In the warmer months, you will enjoy an outdoors breakfast, serenaded by the birds. Mint juleps, garnished with homegrown mint, are served in mason jars that once were used for Piney Grove moonshine. Your hosts also offer a nice selection of Virginia wine,

cider, and apple brandy.

Outdoor recreation holds several options. You can stroll the colorful gardens or take walks along the nature trail, or venture to the springs. If you are a bird-watcher, you have come to the right place. Swimming, croquet, badminton, and volleyball are also on site.

Joan sews and gardens and is your chef, while Joseph enjoys carpentry, antique cars, and farm animals. Historian Brian likes to point out the museum quality and historical authenticity of their combined restoration efforts. They used the original paint colors and floor finishes, period drapery treatments and floor coverings, and a representative collection of antiques and artifacts to illustrate accurately the history.

The warm Southern hospitality so natural to your hosts here brings back such written comments as the thanks from the president of a Texas-based title insurance company: "My family enjoyed ourselves immensely. Ladysmith was just the house for a warm and cozy family

Thanksgiving. The fresh sheets, mints, warm fires we didn't need to start, fantastic breakfasts in the cozy log room, the plantation tours, and Thanksgiving dinner at Indian Fields Tavern — what wonderful arrangements. Y'all did everything right, the perfect hosts, even the traveling breakfast on Sunday. What a treat!"

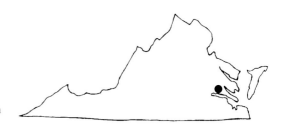

Fares

$100+, first night deposit required, refunded with 2 week notice, check in 4-6 p.m., out by noon

Courtesies

air conditioning, private baths, fireplaces, refrigerators and coffee makers in rooms, TV/VCR available, children welcome, smoking restricted to porches

Brian and CindyRae Gordineer, Joan and Joseph Gordineer

PO Box 1359, Williamsburg VA 23187.
16920 Southall Plantation Lane, Charles City, Va 23030.
804 829-2480. Off Rt 5/Virginia Scenic Byway. From east take Rt 623, go 8 miles. From west take Rt 615, go 7 miles.

PROSPECT HILL PLANTATION INN

two centuries ago...."It begins where the boxwood hedgerow ends. The sun filters through the rare magnolias, tall tulip poplars and giant beeches to the manor house. A few paces away are the slave quarters, log cabin, overseer's house, summer kitchen, smokehouse, carriage house, and groom's quarters. A complete plantation complex in the 18th and 19th centuries."

Today, delightful smells drift from the kitchen and mingle with the sweet, clear country air — your welcome to one of Virginia's finest bed and breakfast inns. Bill and Mireille Sheehan purchased this old property in 1977 and began the extensive renovation to the plantation, now on the National Register of Historic Places and part of the Green Springs National Historic District of Louisa County.

Their son and daughter-in-law, Michael and Laura, have taken over the responsibilities and are the second generation to continue the guest hospitality tradition begun by the Overtons in the 1880s. This quiet refuge from the city emphasizes excellent food and genuine southern hospitality.

The 18th century plantation mixes Greek revival with Victorian architecture, featuring original plantation dependencies converted to guest lodging. Still in a country setting after all these years, the inn is surrounded by working farms and rolling hills. Its local historic district has more than two dozen homes which also pre-date the American Revolution.

Prospect Hill all began when Roger Thompson, one of the original settlers in the westward expansion from Jamestown and Williamsburg, came to this site and constructed a log cabin in 1699 as temporary shelter for his young family. He built a second home, now known as the Overseer's Cottage, in the early 1720s to help house his growing family of

13 children. The boys continued to live in the cabin, which is why today it's called the Boy's Cabin. It later saw use as a slave quarters and then a schoolhouse.

The second home was subsequently used for the plantation office. Around 1732, a barn was built and later converted to the present manor house; this portion today is the parlor and hall. In 1840, two wings were added and the hallway extended for the spiral staircase. The summer kitchen, circa 1730, was built when the Thompson family moved to the manor house. In 1927, the Overton family added the kitchen to the main house.

When Thompson died in 1739, Prospect Hill passed to Samuel Terrill. In 1796 the first slave quarters known as Uncle Guy's House was built. The property was transferred to Terrill's brother; William and his wife spent their last years here and willed the estate to his son Richmond, who married Sally Overton and in 1840 conveyed the home to her half brother, William Overton.

Overton's son William graduated from VMI in 1861 and served under Stonewall Jackson in what Virginians called "the War in Defense of Virginia." Returning to neglected, overgrown fields, he sold tracts of land and accommodated overnight guests in order to make a living.

William married and had three children, who never married but lived out their lives at Prospect Hill. Today the B&B traveler will find lodging in the restored outbuildings with their beamed ceilings, squeaking floors, and crackling fires, as well as in the manor house, where antique furnishings, quilts, and a private veranda overlooking the countryside greet you. You have a wide variety, 13 rooms in all, from which to choose.

The Overton Room with its four

poster queen bed, working fireplace, and jacuzzi more than satisfies your needs. In good weather, breakfast is served on the balcony overlooking the arboretum and cottages. The Carriage House, a suite with a queen bed, working fireplace, jacuzzi, and sitting room, offers pastoral views from the deck off the bedroom.

Each day begins with a full country breakfast served on a tray in your room or in the dining room. Pleasing to any palate are the fresh fruit platter, eggs in pastry with ham or sausage, hot homemade raspberry and praline muffins, and fresh orange juice. You can mingle with the other guests and the Sheehan family at afternoon tea.

Also included in your tariff is a fine dining experience. Dinner begins informally with a glass of wine or cider that you can sip while relaxing in your favorite niche. The dinner bell calls you to a five-course Provencal, candlelit meal in the manor house and begins with the blessing. With advance notice the hosts will cater

to any special diet you might have.

On site pleasures figure a dip in the pool, croquet, badminton, volleyball, and hiking. For some extra special thrills you can arrange carriage rides and hot air ballooning from the inn.

Weddings and receptions are Prospect Hill's forte, and the inn's ample space also accommodates small business retreats well.

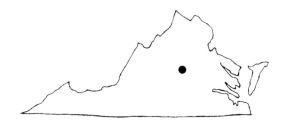

Fares

$155, 10% discount for weekdays, AAA, AARP, deposit required, refunded with 10 day notice, check in 3 p.m., out by 11 a.m.

Courtesies

all rooms air conditioned and with private baths, 13 fireplaces, conference facilities, washer/dryer use, some handicap access, 8 rooms with whirlpools, children welcome, no pets, smoking restricted

Michael and Laura Sheehan

RD 3, Box 430, Trevilians VA 23093.
800 277-0844, 540 967-0844, FAX: 967-0102.
From I-64: Exit 136, 1/4 mile to Zion Crossroads, left on 250 E, 1 mile, left on Rt 613, inn 3 miles on left.

RIVER'D INN

Tucked away in the famous Shenandoah Valley of Virginia, the River'd Inn derives its name from the way the Shenandoah River wraps around this 25-acre retreat at the base of the Massanutten Mountain near Woodstock. When the river rises above the bridge leading to the inn, guests are "river'd in," according to locals. As you relax in the warm, woodsy atmosphere, it's easy to wish the bridge would flood.

Warm weather guests can soak up scenic mountain views from the outdoor pool, the porch swing, or hammock, or while dining on the veranda. In the winter, you can unwind by the fire in the wood-beamed Great Room. Chilly weather shows off some of the River'd Inn's best assets — twelve working fireplaces.

Guests will enjoy all the services of a fine inn. In the evening , quiet dining is highlighted by the six-course, French-based dinner prepared and served by professionally trained staff. Three elegant dining rooms, each with its own distinctive fireplace and intimate seating for no more than 10 guests, provides a rich, warm atmosphere imbued by linen, china, silver, soft candlelight, fresh-cut flowers, and an impressive selection of wines, beers, and spirits.

Contemporary hospitality will add special charm to your visit. The innkeepers have taken care to combine the Victorian style with modern convenience. Centrally heated and air conditioned, each guest room contains selected antiques, an 18th century fireplace or Franklin stove, queen beds, and private baths — two featuring jacuzzi tubs. A third whirlpool tub is also available.

Within short driving distances are the New Market Battlefield and Civil War Museum; Massanutten and Bryce ski resorts; Shenandoah National Park; Luray, Shenandoah and Endless Caverns; Belle Grove

Plantation; and Wayside Theatre. Wine connoisseurs will relish the tastings of fine Virginia wines at numerous area vineyards, while antique buffs will delight in the treasures to be found at many nearby shops.

When you drive into River'd Inn from Route 11, you have traveled what is known as Old Valley Pike, which during the Civil War was vital to General Jackson's foot cavalry in the Campaign of 1862. Numerous locations in the town of Woodstock served as offices, headquarters, and meeting places for soldiers and high-ranking commanders.

General Sheridan's famous telegraph of "The Burning of the Valley" was made from the old Shenandoah House on Woodstock's Main Street: "I have destroyed over 2,000 barns filled with wheat, burned over 70 mills filled with grain and flour....I have made the Shenandoah Valley of Virginia so bare that a crow flying over it would have to carry its knapsack."

Many battles were fought very close to the River'd Inn, including the Battle of Tom's Brook, Fisher's Hill, New Market, Cedar Creek, and Hupp's Hill. Local men served in the Stonewall Brigade and the Muhlenberg Rifles. The Woodstock Museum can fill you in.

If you want to view the Seven Bends of the Shenandoah River, visit the Woodstock Tower. You are in the heart of the Shenandoah Valley, and although it was devastated during the Civil War, you will revel in its pastoral beauty today.

And so it is, that each season at the River'd Inn offers its own lure. No matter when you come, a warm welcome from innkeepers Alan and Diana Edwards awaits you.

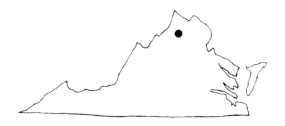

Fares

$110+, credit card guarantee, 72 hour cancellation policy, check in 2 p.m, out by 11 a.m.

Courtesies

central heat and air, private baths, some with jacuzzis, refrigerator use, whirlpool, children over 12 welcome, smoking permitted with some restriction, fine selection of beer, wine, and spirits, in-room flowers and champagne available, picnicking, hiking, fishing on property

Alan and Diana Edwards

*1972 Artz Road, Woodstock VA 22664.
800 637-4561, 540 459-5369.
From I-81 S: Exit 291 (Tom's Brook), onto Rt 11 S, left on Rt 663, go 2.1 miles. From I-81 N: Exit 283 (Woodstock), onto Rt 11 N, right onto Rt 663, go 2.1 miles.*

SAMPSON EAGON INN

The personal comfort of their guests takes priority for Frank and Laura Mattingly at the Sampson Eagon Inn in Staunton. A warmly elegant decor, relaxed and sincere hospitality, and consideration given to the little details further describe their innkeeping. When you enter the doors you are able to experience a rich past with the pleasures and conveniences of today.

The inn is well-appointed throughout with carefully-chosen period antiques from the innkeepers' personal collection interspersed with handcrafted reproductions. Authentic oriental rugs accent the interiors. The queen canopy beds, all very distinctive, are in a class by themselves, especially the perfectly proportioned, arched canopy bed.

Guests will find the bedrooms spacious with sitting areas, comfortable furniture, good lighting, firm custom-made mattresses, quality linens, and both down and non-allergic bedding. Large, modern baths join each room. Towels are thick, and the water stays hot! Plush carpet and solid masonry walls ensure total quiet and privacy.

Guest rooms are equipped with a TV and VCR, beverage service, an alarm clock, and an assortment of reading materials, including menus from all the area restaurants. You will relish the turn-down service and gourmet chocolates placed by your bed. A refrigerator and basket of personal items are available for guests to use.

The Eagon Master Suite comes with a sun porch outfitted in wicker and with a large private bath designed by the noted Virginia architect, T. J. Collins. Many of the five rooms look out to views of Historic Staunton; one of the guest quarters is on the main floor and features a spa-type shower.

Window treatments and bed hangings are appropriately fashioned in designer fabrics. Artwork and objets d'art individualize the decor of each room. The remarkable feat of the hosts is the pleasing manner in which they reflect the 150-year-old home's several phases of architecture — combining design elements from the federal, American empire, Victorian, colonial, and Greek revival periods.

A state of the art heating and cooling system maintains comfortable, even temperatures year round. Business travelers have not been forgotten in the amenities of the house. A phone and fax are available for their use.

After six years of looking for the right place, Frank, a former hospital administrator, and Laura, an early-retired college administrator, forsook Washington, D.C., "existence" to open up this B&B in the quiet Shenandoah Valley, where things are happening but at a quality of life pace. So it's important to them to give their guests a really nice experience. They make every effort to provide a hospitable atmosphere, from offering personalized information regarding area attractions and travel assistance, to shuttle pickup and adjusting breakfast times.

They will be sensitive to your dietary concerns; just speak up. Their check in and out times also flow with your particular needs. Your hosts are even flexible enough to help you out of a laundry jam!

Guests have access to a refrigerator, small library, a collection of games, and a selection of videos. The parlor, where light streams in through floor-to-ceiling windows, provides a good sitting area where you can read or plan a day of sightseeing.

Breakfast is a real treat and includes seasonal fresh fruit, coffee ground that morning, teas, several breads (like Laura's tasty lemon walnut), and specialty entrees, such as Grand Marnier souffle pancakes and pecan Belgian waffles — all served royally with English china, Waterford crystal, and family

sterling. A continental breakfast is available for those who choose to sleep late.

Located in the fashionable Gospel Hill District, a Virginia Historic Landmark, the Sampson Eagon Inn is adjacent to Woodrow Wilson's birthplace. Mary Baldwin College is within walking distance and Staunton's Victorian downtown is two blocks away. Other magnificent old residences surround the inn.

During several ownerships the 1840 town mansion underwent five periods of updating and enlarging. The colonial revival stage removed many Italianate and Victorian features, including the wraparound porch, which was replaced along with restoration of the original portico during a subsequent ownership. For their deluxe restoration efforts from 1990 to 1992, the current owners received Historic Staunton Foundation's Annual Preservation Award.

Extensive exterior repairs were also required to restore the limestone walls encircling the property and the ornamental ironwork on top. The Mattinglys have carefully enhanced the landscape with mature evergreens to complement the 150-year-old

boxwoods that define the property.

When it comes to the outdoors, your hosts are just as tuned in to what guests want.

Fares

$85-$99, cash, personal and travelers checks, credit cards accepted, night's deposit required, full refund with 3 day notice, midweek corporate rate available, 2 night minimum during holidays and selected weekends, check in 4-8 p.m., out by 11 a.m. .

Courtesies

all rooms air conditioned with canopied beds, private baths, sitting areas, individual TV/VCRs; beverages and snacks, access to in-room phone, washer/dryer use by request, exercise facilities close by, non-smoking environment, no pets, gift certificates

Frank and Laura Mattingly

*238 E Beverley St, Staunton VA 24401.
800 597-9722, 540 886-8200.
From I-81: Exit 222 or 225, follow signs to Woodrow Wilson Birthplace.*

SILVER THATCH INN

With room names like the George Washington, Thomas Jefferson, James Madison, James Monroe, William Henry Harrison, John Tyler, and Zachary Taylor, you know you have landed at an inn in the heart of a state that has given birth to more U.S. Presidents than any other. The two-century-old establishment could not be a more appropriate place for an American history lesson.

Built on the site of an Indian village, the inn has seen life as a Revolutionary War prisoners' camp, boys' school, tobacco plantation, melon farm, home to a University of Virginia (UVA) dean, a restaurant, and since 1984 a lodging for travelers. The building itself traces its roots back to 1780, when Hessian soldiers, who were made prisoners at the battle of Saratoga and marched down from New York, built a two-story, log barracks in which to live. Today, the white clapboard structure is one of the oldest in Central Virginia and is called the Hessian Room.

The center part of the inn was built in 1812 for the boys' school and now is a dining area. In 1937, the UVA dean added a wing for his library, and, in 1984, a cottage was built to make way for B&B guest rooms. As its name connotes, the inn offers dining as well as sleeping quarters. Three dining rooms and a bar serve on- and off-premise guests by candlelight Tuesday through Saturday evenings from 5:30 until 9 p.m.

Gourmet chefs prepare modern American cuisine par excellence, often using fresh produce from local farms. House specialties include tender veal, poultry and seafood dishes, and vegetarian selections. Choice desserts and award winning domestic and Virginia wines cap the fine dining.

A continental breakfast, served in the cheerful sunroom, comes with your stay. Freshly baked muffins, assorted cereals, fresh fruit (like melons garnished with strawberries, in season), and morning beverages make up the fare. Upon arrival you are offered complimentary wine, beer, and soft drinks.

Each guest room has its own personalized decor and a private bath, and some rooms are blessed with fireplaces. Three bedrooms reside in the main building, while four others are in the cottage. The premium colonial inn is furnished with well-chosen antiques and quality reproductions.

From the flower-lined brick walkway, tall elms, scattering of dogwoods, and charming courtyards outside to the deep, rich tones of the decorating schemes inside, you have country elegance and comfort at its combined best. Cascading drapes of imported fabrics, handsome quilts, and bathroom amenities galore complete the picture.

Silver Thatch puts you in the middle of Mr. Jefferson's historic country and minutes away from UVA, Monticello and its newly refurbished gardens, Michie Tavern, James Monroe's Ash Lawn, and James Madison's Montpelier. Afton Mountain, where the Skyline Drive goes north and the Blue Ridge Parkway heads south, is 20 minutes west, near Wintergreen, which offers skiing. You can ramble the back roads of colonial America, enjoy fox hunting and steeplechases, tour wineries, or search for antiques.

When all that's exhausted, you can collapse into a cozy niche back at the inn or take a relaxing swim in the pool if it's summertime. If you love the outdoors, you will find plenty of opportunities for hiking, biking, skiing, golfing, and fishing.

Innkeepers Vince and Rita Scoffone left their native Arlington, VA, area to operate Silver Thatch Inn. Vince spent 30 years in banking and Rita was a part-time

medical assistant and mother to three children. They caution that in making reservations you should remember that the inn fills up a year in advance for special weekends at UVA.

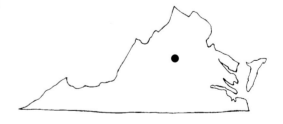

Fares

$110-$135, credit card guarantee only, refunded with 2 day notice, check in 2 p.m., out by 11 a.m.

Courtesies

air conditioning, private baths, fireplaces in 4 of 7 rooms, conference facilities for 20, washer/dryer use on request, handicap access being developed, well-behaved children over 4 welcome, totally smoke-free

Vince and Rita Scoffone

3001 Hollymead Dr, Charlottesville VA 22901.
804 978-4686, FAX: 973-6156.
6 miles north of intersection of Rt 29 N and Rt 250 Bypass, .3 mile on Rt 1520.

SLEEPY
HOLLOW FARM

In this day and age of diet and environmentally conscious citizens, the pure, delicious spring water alone is sufficient to keep you coming back to Sleepy Hollow Farm. Not to mention the Dolley Madison hospitality of innkeepers Beverley Allison and Dorsey Allison Comer. Or the commanding landscapes of surrounding horse, cattle, and sheep farms. So many B&Bs are not equipped to handle children, but this one is!

It should be no surprise that you can only get to Sleepy Hollow one way, via a Scenic Byway, Virginia Route 231, a historic road that has been used for centuries and over, which colonial and Civil War troops of both sides marched. The scenic country road has retained its rural character after all these years and winds through some of Virginia's lushest hills.

The red Sleepy Hollow mailbox that shouts "Welcome" signals that you are here. If you miss that, look for a green barn with a very red roof, a gazebo, pond, and brick house snoozing under trees in a sleepy hollow. They are verification that you have arrived at the hollow's namesake.

Generations of farm families have lived in the simple farmhouse. Now it attracts a wide spectrum of guests, including many international sojourners.

It remains a mystery who built the first dwelling or when, but the foundation suggests late 1700s. In the 1850s a two-story, three-room clapboard house was built in front of the earlier building. Later a shed kitchen was constructed, and in 1940 two side rooms were added and the whole farmhouse bricked over. The small slave cabin of chestnut has been renovated and a two-story addition put on.

Two terraces, a pair of front and side porches, a croquet lawn, and cozy bedrooms promise you some low-key moments of relaxation. Homemade cookies, pie or cake are available any time on the formal dining room sideboard, with accompanying hot or cold beverages. Each morning you will enjoy a country breakfast in the large, sunny, porch dining room. One day you might enjoy fried apples, biscuits, bacon or sausage, eggs, fruit compote, juice, and coffee or tea. A herb quiche, baked tomatoes, fried potatoes, muffins, poached pears, juice, and coffee or tea might start another day. The herbs, vegetables, and flowers used at Sleepy Hollow are grown on the property.

Your hosts do not mind sharing their recipes. Beverley's natural talent for being such a gracious host reflects her love for mission field work. She served in Central and South America and remains actively associated with many Episcopal missions. She is currently Executive Director of an organization that supports Our Little Roses Home for Girls in Honduras.

Dorsey is the keeper of the animals — three dogs, two cats, two ducks — and the books. She lives close by with her husband and two daughters, all who also help in many ways on this family farm.

The six guest rooms have private baths. Upstairs in the main house is a two-bedroom suite that nicely accommodates families. A smaller bedroom, the Ghost Chamber, once frequented by a Civil War nurse, overlooks the pond. Col. Mosby was also once a guest at Sleepy Hollow.

Downstairs, the Master Room with a four-poster bed and small dressing room is a favorite with travelers. The Squire Room with a queen bed, large fireplace, and whirlpool tub attracts honeymooners.

Out back, the Chestnut Cottage accommodates two suites, both with downstairs sitting rooms. One features a deck entrance, full kitchen, and Franklin wood burning stove; the other has a fireplace. Upstairs bedrooms have double beds and make for a

quaint getaway.

The prettiest dining room anywhere overlooks the herb garden and distant rolling Piedmont. Floral accents add a dash of color to the room. Your innkeepers have furnished their delightful abode, which was blessed in 1959, with antiques and accessories from generations past.

The outside playing field is perfect for small private parties, BBQs, croquet, badminton, or Frisbee. Rooms in both the main house and cottage are well suited for small business meetings or retreats.

Sleepy Hollow is one of the few inns catering to children. Baby cribs and high chairs are available. One of Beverley's granddaughters will baby sit. A play area with swings, sandbox, and lots of space await youthful energies. Farm tours can be arranged at a local dairy or sheep farm.

If you want to sightsee some Civil War sites, you are near the Wilderness Battlefield, where Stonewall Jackson's amputated arm is buried — a history lesson your children won't forget.

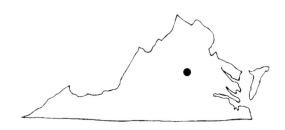

Fares

$65-$110, night's deposit required or credit card guarantee, refunded with 1 week notice and during peak season 2 weeks, whole house and cottage reservations for parties, check in 3 p.m.

Courtesies

air conditioning, fans, iron and board, private baths, children welcome, ask about pet arrangements

Beverley Allison and Dorsey Allison Comer

16280 Blue Ridge Turnpike, Gordonsville VA 22942.
800 215-4804, FAX: 832-2515.
90 miles from Washington, D.C.; 67 miles from Richmond.
On Rt 231 between Gordonsville and Somerset.

℘A wine and fruit basket exquisitely await in the rooms for guests stopping over at Steeles Tavern Manor, a relaxing, romantic getaway. "The sweetest B&B ever," is the way one guest described his stay.

Your innkeepers specialize in creating a comfortable atmosphere for couples who seek to be alone together. If you feel like getting out and about, you will revel in the wonderful towns of Lexington and Staunton, as well as enjoy other sightseeing, antiquing, shopping, and visiting the local winery.

Confederate generals Robert E. Lee and Stonewall Jackson had their homes, colleges, churches, and final resting places in Lexington.

Birding, fishing, walking, hiking, reading, and just relaxing are yours for the asking at the manor.

Since 1781, a Steeles Tavern home in the tiny village of Steeles Tavern has provided lodging to Shenandoah Valley travelers passing along historic Rt. 11, also called the Lee Highway. In 1831, John Steele, a descendent of the original settler David, let his good friend and neighbor Cyrus McCormick give his first public exhibition of the reaper in a field of oats in front of the tavern.

In 1857, James Gibbs, who lived one and a half miles from the village, invented the machine known today as the Wilcox Gibbs sewing machine. Most Americans do not know that little, rural Steeles Tavern is the birthplace of two highly significant labor saving devices of the 20th century — the reaper and the sewing machine!

A new home built in 1916 is the current Steeles Tavern Manor. Innkeepers Eileen Hoernlein, who kept the Bay Head Gables Inn in New Jersey several years, and husband Bill, who wanted a change of pace after working in Jersey for 39 years, extensively restored the home in 1994 and a year later opened it as their B&B.

STEELES TAVERN MANOR

The home nestles on 55 acres of peaceful countryside with a creek, springs, pond, and views of the Blue Ridge panorama. With names like Dahlia, Wisteria, and Rose Garden, it is not difficult to envision the guest rooms. Among the five is a Hyacinth Room that elicits true elegance for a memorable escape. It is filled with a king sleigh bed, cozy sitting area, and two person whirlpool tub.

The Buttercup Room turns back the hands of time where antique oak furnishings complement the comfortable quarters. The queen bed, antique quilts, lace, and fireplace enchant you.

You awake to fresh coffee at your door. Breakfast hour begins at 8:30 and continues to 9:30 in the dining room, or you may choose to have it delivered to your room. The menu, which varies some daily but often has guests helping themselves to seconds, covers juice, fresh fruit, sweet cake, and an entree of eggs, potatoes, meat, and biscuits. Your hosts are interested in knowing any special diet needs you may have and are flexible if you want to request a special serving time.

The guest refrigerator is stocked with soda, and the ubiquitous cookie jar stays loaded. Afternoon tea is served between 4 and 5 p.m.

The manor's meals are all homemade, including the baked goods. With reservations, you may have dinner on Friday and Saturday evenings.

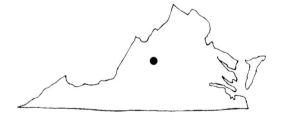

Fares

$95-$130+, credit cards, reservations preferred,min. weekend stay in May and October, night's depositor 50% of stay — which ever is greater, refund 10 days prior less $15 service charge, check in 3 p.m, out by 11 a.m.

Courtesies

central air, bedrooms have ceiling fans and private baths, gas fireplaces in some rooms, private guest refrigerator available, TV/ VCR in all rooms, video library available, two-person whirlpool in two rooms, guest phone, smoking outside only

Eileen and Bill Hoernlein

PO Box 39, Hwy 11, Steeles Tavern VA 24476.
800 743-8666, FAX: 540 377-5937.
From I-81: Exit 205 Steeles Tavern, east on Rt 606 for 1.5 miles, right onto Rt 11, quick left into driveway.

SYCAMORE HILL HOUSE AND GARDENS

aking every advantage of the spectacular panoramic views of the Blue Ridge Mountains, Sycamore Hill House and Gardens is unique for its glass walls and many large windows. Built from Virginia fieldstone, the large secluded home sits 1,043 feet high atop 52 acres near historic Washington, Virginia, just minutes away from the Skyline Drive.

This B&B was started in 1987 by Kerri and Stephen Wagner, who traded the urban stress of Washington, D.C., for the rural tranquility of Rappahannock County. Stephen, an internationally-published illustrator, continues to pursue his art, and his original pieces fill the inn. You may even find some paintings or prints for sale, along with Stephen's original greeting cards. Kerri left her career as a registered agricultural lobbyist and has poured her energies into creating and running the bed and breakfast full time.

Kerri and Steve share their prized possession with B&B guests who quickly fall in love with some of the most spectacular mountain views to be had. The rainbow at the end of the mile-long drive up Menefee Mountain is Sycamore Hill House itself, designed with a semicircular, glass-wall living room and 65-foot veranda facing the Blue Ridge Mountains. Guests most enjoy sitting in big rocking chairs on the curved veranda. As far as the eye can see is undisturbed countryside and majestic mountains. Also vying for your attention are the many artistically landscaped gardens that embellish the grounds.

The annual and perennial flower beds, including one with some 2,500 irises, provide fresh cut flowers for the colorful arrangements throughout the house. The gardens also attract birds, butterflies, and other wildlife. Profuse plantings of daffodils, zinnias, irises, daylilies, columbine, and peonies put Sycamore Hill House and Gardens in a class by itself.

Specially designed birdhouses are strategically placed to attract nesting bluebirds. A red garden just outside the front door provides a feast for hummingbirds. Other species of birds join ranks at the various feeders and suet stations, while red fox, white-tailed deer, or a wild turkey are just as apt to cross your path. It is the decade of the environment, and this is one place you can certainly appreciate the wildlife. You will not be surprised to learn that Sycamore Hill is a certified National Wildlife habitat.

Spring, when the hundreds of dogwood and redbud trees are in bloom and the meadows full of buttercups, may be the loveliest time of the year on the mountain. Crisp fall days are equally delightful, when the mountains and fields are painted with the brilliant autumn palette.

Companion interests propelled Steve and Kerri to raise herbs and vegetables, which are incorporated into the inn's menus and supplied to local restaurants. In the summer, you may find yourself heading home with some fat, organic tomatoes or a pint of the couple's fiery four-pepper salsa.

Furnished in an eclectic contemporary style, the house's interior reflects a clean, open design, especially emphasized by the enormous windows. Perhaps the best touch of all, next to Steve's art, is Kerri's famous greenery — lush African violets, exotic orchids, huge weeping fig trees, and many other plants that appear in every corner of the sunny rooms.

The guest floor has blond hardwood floors and handsome oriental rugs throughout. You may choose from three elegant and tasteful rooms, each with a queen bed, large private bath, and mountain views. There are sitting/reading areas in all guest rooms, and always plants and fresh flowers. The Master Bedroom,

done in pale green with rose accents, features a waist-high four-poster bed, six-foot picture window, dressing room, and full bath with twin sinks. The Peach Room, with a brass bed, offers huge windows on three sides and bookcases filled with novels, guidebooks, and other reading materials. Fresh cookies, bedtime mints, and brandy complete your feeling of luxury.

Breakfast is a real treat, and served outdoors when weather permits. French toast with local raspberries or blueberries is a favorite, served with real maple syrup, fresh-squeezed orange juice, and specially-blended coffee. Some mornings you might feast on baked apples, crab quiche, or an apple souffle.

Five-star dining and other excellent restaurants are within several miles. Also nearby are Luray Caverns, Old Rag Mountain, Skyline Drive, antiques, arts and crafts, golf, tennis, ballooning, canoeing, and horseback riding. There are excellent vineyards that offer tours and tastings, plus a variety of Christmas tree farms

and pick-your-own establishments with strawberries, apples, peaches, and other local produce.

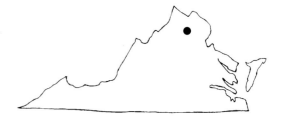

Fares

$100-$155, midweek business discounts, one night deposit by Visa/Mastercard or check required within 5 days of reservation, refunded less $20 with week notice, check in 2 p.m., out by 11 a.m.

Courtesies

air conditioning, ceiling fans, stereo or TV in some bedrooms, stereo and TV in common rooms, game table, refrigerator use, breakfast at 9 a.m., handicap access, no smoking, no pets or children under 12

Kerri and Stephen Wagner

110 Menefee Mountain Lane, Washington VA 22747.
540 675-3046.
66 miles west of Washington, D.C., 1 mile east of Washington, VA, at intersection of Rt 211 and Rt 683.

THISTLE HILL

A linear cascading of architecture, this inviting B&B blends right in against the hillside in a park-like setting and parallels a stream that traverses the 10 acres. Not surprising because of the inn's name, thistle blooms abundantly from late June to early July and like a magnetic field attracts swarms of butterflies. Bird feeders and flowering plants bring equal numbers of gold finches, hummingbirds, and cardinals. An ornamental fish pond with a fountain, waterlilies, and goldfish lends another note of grace.

The country comfortable home, near the sleepy crossroads of unheard of Boston, Virginia, is situated on the morning side of the Blue Ridge Mountains and a stone's throw from Old Rag Mountain. It was built about 30 years ago and has a newly completed Great Room with cathedral ceiling, balcony, fireplace, stained-glass windows, and French doors leading to the long front porch and deck.

The colonial style home features a gazebo and two cottages. Guests may choose from five sleeping accommodations. The Char Mar Room's prize is the Amish quilt in a wedding ring pattern much bolder than usually seen. Wide-board pine floors softened with oriental rugs, a handsome queen poster canopy bed, fine antiques, interesting collectibles, and deck leading to a hot tub in the back yard are bound to please any over nighter. A free-standing fireplace is in the master plan. Meanwhile, individual heat control allows you to regulate heat.

Little Thistle House will charm you. This honeymoon cottage with a large bedroom-sitting area comes outfitted with wing back chairs beside a fireplace, a queen sleigh bed with half canopy, antique corner cupboard, dresser, dropleaf table, and carved-back chairs. Oriental rugs garnish wall-to-wall carpeting. The accent here is the oversize bath's garden tub with an overhead skylight.

The crowning glory of this B&B might be its food, thanks to your innkeeper couple, Charles A. Wilson and Marianne W. Topjian-Wilson. Although breakfast comes with your lodging, on a separate tab you can enjoy a gourmet dinner. A retired pharmacist-physician, Charles studied with Marcella Hazan in Italy and as a young man cooked for Hot Shoppes. He maintains an extensive wine cellar with French, Italian, German, California, and local wines.

Your breakfast table is set with morning beverages, fruit, cereal, homemade breads or muffins, an egg dish, and waffles. Carrot-walnut muffins, Amish bacon, and omelets encasing mushrooms, tomatoes, alfalfa sprouts, sour cream, and onion bits are sure to whet your appetite. Corned beef hash and out-of-the-oven raisin bread may nourish you another morning.

A afternoon tea you will relish as much: sweets and savory munchies served in the gazebo during summer or inside wherever guests prefer during the cooler months. Dinner is by reservation and available to guests and the public at reasonable charges. What a feast! Samplings from the fairly extensive menu (with translations from the Italian) run from cream of peanut soup, spinach and feta salad, grilled swordfish, and marinated grilled vegetables to roasted duck, chicken sauteed with sausage, grilled eggplant, veal sauteed in wine sauce, and scrodfish dijon.

Perhaps the highlights of your stay at Thistle Hall are the hosts themselves, jacks of all trades with burgeoning interests. Charles, who hails from Pennsylvania, met Marianne, a New Yorker and non-practicing family therapist, in Florida. Charles has traveled and sailed extensively; he and

Marianne lived on a boat for a year anticipating a trip through the Panama Canal. Charles sailed his last boat, a 47-foot steel hull, from England to Florida! Marianne is active in the Bed and Breakfast Association of Virginia and numerous other travel organizations.

Horseshoes, croquet, bocce, and volleyball are played at Thistle Hall. And if you want to tour the countryside, some mountain bikes are ready and waiting. There is even an antique shop on the premises.

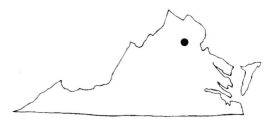

Fares

$95-$145, 15% midweek discount, first night deposit required, refunded with 1 week notice, check in 3 p.m., out by 11 a.m.

Courtesies

air conditioning, fans, private baths, fireplaces, personal heat controls, facilities for small conferences and receptions, refrigerator use, phone and TV in room upon request, laundry service available, hot tub in back yard, children welcome, smoking outside, official greeter "Ace" regrets no pets accepted

Charles and Marianne Wilson

5541 Sperryville Pike, Boston VA 22713.
540 987-9142, FAX: 987-9122.
Rt 522 between Culpeper and Sperryville, 8 miles south of caution light in Sperryville.

WIDOW KIP'S

he 1830 restored homestead sets on seven rural acres and offers a bird's-eye view of the Shenandoah River just 50 yards away. Many splendors of the Shenandoah Valley, George Washington-Jefferson National Forest, and the Massanutten Mountains are within minutes of this serene hideaway.

Three Civil War museums and battlefields are located in the vicinity. Re-enactments are held every year on May 15. More than 300 Civil War graves occupy Mt. Jackson's confederate cemetery. Many skirmishes took place on a daily basis in the region.

There are five guest rooms in the main home, where you'll discover top-notch antiques throughout the interiors. The appealing decorations capture the Victorian era.

The first floor has a common room, where guests can play backgammon or checkers before a friendly fire. All bedrooms have original wood burning fireplaces and private baths.

The restful, airy Wildflower Room on the second floor overlooks the mountains and has a four-poster canopy-bed covered by a locally-crafted quilt. Mauve tones highlight the decor, along with a well stocked bookcase, rocker, and other comforts. The Morning Glory Room, with a handcarved Victorian bed and Empire dresser and arm chairs, basks in cozy Williamsburg blues.

The inn extends its offerings beyond the main home to two cottages. Sow's Ear, which amazingly once was a henhouse, has a porch, cozy bedroom, and generous bath. It will remind you of an English cottage. Silk Purse, the other courtyard cottage and a former wash house, has two bedrooms, kitchen, porch, and bath.

Host Bob is retired from the world of marketing in Manhattan.

Betty, who raised four children, enjoys cooking. Because they both love people and entertaining they now are in the B&B business, which Bob describes as "like having company 24 hours a day." Likewise, guests depart with pleasurable experiences and leave behind such comments as "what a perfect weekend," "you have set a standard of professional excellence and warm hospitality," and "don't change a thing, we will be back." One couple returns monthly!

The friendly, family-style breakfast includes fresh juice, baked apples—of course, when you're in the heart of Virginia's apple country—other fruits, homemade sausage, homemade stuffed French toast and syrups, waffles with peaches and cream, apple dapple cake, and crumb cake.

Other refreshments available during your stay are hot cider, iced tea, lemonade, sodas, non-alcoholic beverages, and cookies. When you venture out you may want to pack a picnic. Guests are always welcome in the Widow Kip's kitchen.

It's easy to slow down to a snail's pace at this tranquil home, where you can enjoy some good book reading on the side porch. An in-ground swimming pool out back always proves restful and relaxing.

Weekend auctions, hiking, horseback riding, canoeing and rafting, fishing, golf, downhill skiing, tennis, craft fairs, caverns, vineyards, bikes, and picnics will vie for your time. Orkney Springs Outdoor Music Festival runs from May to September.

Bikes are provided for a carefree ride through the apple orchard or over to the Shenandoah Caverns nearby. You can also experience a pleasant ride through the covered bridge at Meems Bottom.

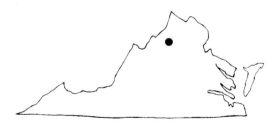

Fares

$60+, reservations needed for 3-day holidays and local college parents' weekend, deposit by credit card or check, 5 day notice for refund, check in 3 p.m., out by 11 a.m.

Courtesies

air conditioning, fans, conference facilities for groups of 10 or less, refrigerator use, young children and pets permitted in cottages, bikes available, no smoking

Betty and Bob Luse

*355 Orchard Dr, Mt. Jackson VA 22842.
800 478-8714, 540 477-2400.
From I-81: Exit 273 Mt. Jackson East to Rt 11 S, go 1.3 miles, right onto Rt 263, left after overpass onto 698, second house on left, entrance on Mill Creek Lane.*

WILLOW GROVE INN

ormer neighbor of yesteryear and famous hostess Dolly Madison had nothing over people-loving, fun-loving Angela Mulloy, who runs Willow Grove Inn with her family. This is a friendly place, where you can relax, enjoy good food, and have fun yourself.

Willow Grove also merits architectural and historic repute. Like many early prominent homes, it began as a simple federal-style frame building in 1778 and received improvements as the owners prospered. Today the stately manor house is an important example of the influence of Thomas Jefferson on the central piedmont area. The inn's classical-revival addition with a two-story columned portico was built to Thomas Jefferson's design by the same workmen who completed the Jefferson-designed University of Virginia.

The plantation, which survived both the Revolutionary and Civil Wars, is a Virginia Historic Landmark and is listed on the National Register of Historic Places. Generals Wayne and Muhlenberg camped here when America fought for her independence. Confederate General A. P. Hill briefly headquartered at the mansion. Telltale signs have been the buttons and belt buckles from soldier uniforms, breastworks, visible trenches, and a cannon ball that was removed from the eaves.

Although carefully preserved and impeccably decorated with personally-selected American and English antiques, the home is truly lived in. Honest-to-goodness squeaky, old pine floors remind you that you are sleeping in the pages of a history book. Each of the seven rooms and two suites in the manor house are named for a Virginia-born U.S. president and furnished with period pieces popular during his lifetime. The third floor sitting room and adjoining veranda make for a super hideaway, while the second floor reception hall and front and back verandas are other stowaway niches. Four antebellum dependencies - a summer kitchen, weaver's cottage, schoolhouse and gardener's cottage house additional accommodations.

Wake up in the morning to a newspaper and starter-breakfast outside your door. The full plantation breakfast downstairs may lead you to dispense with lunch and then end your day at the inn with a candlelight dinner accompanied by soft piano music.

Willow Grove's restaurant serves lunch and dinner. Three dining rooms exude their own personalities. The casual Clark's Tavern, an 18th century English pub that was once the root cellar, today dishes up steaming soups, crab fritters, smoked trout cakes, fluffy omelets, hearty sandwiches, and more. Formal elegance reigns over the Jefferson Library and the Dolley Madison Dining Room, where the lavish Sunday brunch or dinner is worth a trip from anywhere and where the wine menu reads like a Blue Chip stock list.

The source of all this good food is Willow Grove's chefs, who prepare new Virginia cuisine based on what's available locally — rabbit, free-range veal, hatchery-raised trout from Rappahannock County, and seasonal vegetables from the garden. In addition to more than eight kinds of tomatoes, 30 different herbs, and 10 varieties of greens, Willow Grove even grows its own raspberries, pears, peaches, walnuts, pecans, and chestnuts.

If you have come to the inn for simple R & R, you will be tempted to stake out a fireplace and curl up with a good book. If you want a little more action, you will enjoy a picnic by the creek or a round of bocce, badminton, or croquet. If you can manage to slip away from the serene 37 acres, you will not want to miss neighboring

Montpelier, Madison's lifelong home. Other sightseeing sites abound, as do golden opportunities for canoeing, fishing, hiking, and cycling.

You just might want to mark the pre-Christmas season down on your calendar for a visit. When Angela opened her family inn she started a tradition of hosting a festival the first weekend in December to herald the holiday season. A pair of oxen will be waiting to cart you around like rural gentry.

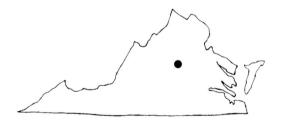

Fares

$95-$155, deposit required, refunded with 10 day notice, flexible check in and out times

Courtesies

private baths, fireplaces, ideal for executive gatherings up to 40, children welcome

Angela Mulloy

14079 Plantation Way, Orange VA 22960.
800 949-1778, 540-672 5982, FAX: 672-3674
From Rt 29 S: Rt 15 S, 15 miles to entrance on left.

WOODRUFF
HOUSE

hef owned and operated, the Woodruff House specializes in, as you might expect, gourmet cuisine. Not only does the B&B have its own wine label, but all of its endearing encumbrances will lure you back — satisfying fireside candlelit parlors, two garden spas heated all seasons, and pleasant outdoor porches in the best of southern traditions.

Six guest accommodations feature private bathrooms and working fireplaces. One of the more special quarters, the Log Cabin Suite, occupies the whole top floor of the house with wooden beams and turrets, an antique brass bed, and brass chandelier.

Handsomely restored antiques, oriental rugs, heirloom silver, china, and artful period decor earmark the interiors with distinction. Fresh flowers lend a defining accent. The soft, intimate touches appeal to honeymooners and anniversary guests, as well as provide the perfect backdrop for small weddings.

Your hosts love to pamper their guests. So you will find coffee at your door in the morning. The hard part is choosing one of the 24 house blends. The ultimate breakfast follows in the candlelit dining room. The chef's creation runs the gamut — maybe fruit topped puffed pancakes with breakfast meats, or the house southern quiche with a special sherry sauce. Evening rates entitle visitors to a sumptuous evening high tea buffet and afternoon tea.

In 1882 the Victorian section of the home was built; it has undergone several transformations. A tall roofline gives Woodruff House its fairytale-like appearance. The original structure was built in the early 1800s as a post and beam cabin and today contains the fireside dining room. During the Civil War, the upstairs loft, legend has it, was used in the underground railroad. In 1990 the current owners purchased the building, began renovating it for an inn, and gave the home their name.

Woodruff House is located in Luray, which is a small town like Lake Woebegone, where time forgot. Luray is squirreled away one valley over from the Shenandoah Valley, where you would not think there would be anything!

Your hosts supply complimentary bicycles, which is a neat way to explore the charms of Luray, as well as canoes for the nearby lake. You will enjoy the flowering gardens and park benches right at the inn. Especially delightful are the fountain pond and gazebo-covered spa.

Lucas has had many years of fine culinary experience, and Deborah comes from a background in public relations and hotel management. Some evenings they stage wine tastings and Murder Mysteries.

While you are in Luray you will want to visit the caverns, which also has one of the best car museums in the nation. It is crammed full with some incredibly fine old vintage models. Luray has a golf course, where you may spy the resident muskrat on the 17th hole. Your hosts can steer you to swimming holes, horseback riding, vineyards, or specialty antique shops.

You are well positioned to take off for the Shenandoah National Park, the George Washington-Jefferson National Forest, New Market Battlefield (a private museum that tells the Civil War story perhaps better than any other!), and Massanutten and Bryce Resorts (where wintertime spells downhill skiing).

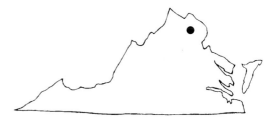

Fares

$98 (includes breakfast for two, evening high tea buffet, afternoon tea), discounts, night's deposit or credit card guarantee, refunded with 7 day notice, holidays require 2-3 month advanced reservations, check in 3 p.m., out by noon

Courtesies

air conditioning, fans, private baths, fireplaces, small conference facilities, TV in room, washer/dryer use, whirlpool, well-behaved children welcome weekdays with reservations, pets kenneled, smoking outdoors only

Deborah and Lucas Woodruff

330 Mechanic St, Luray VA 22835.
540 743-1494; FAX, call first.
From I-66 W: Exit 6 at Front Royal, turn right onto Rt 340 S, merge onto Rt 340 Bus. at Luray, right onto Rt 211 Bus. (Main St), right onto Lee St, go 1 block. From I-81: Exit 264 at New Market, take Rt 211 E then Rt 211 Bus. to Luray, left onto Lee St.

ABOUT THE AUTHORS

Lynn Matthews Davis loves her native state of Virginia — its magnificent outdoors, the history tales tucked in every fold, adventures to be had ad infinitum, and heaps of warmhearted people from shining sea to blue ridge mountains. She was born with a spirit to travel and collects lore like a squirrel does acorns. In the early days of her career she wrote travel articles for the Baltimore-Washington International Airport and later worked with the Virginia Division of Tourism on projects; she served on the Governor's Blue Ridge Region Tourism Task Force. At Virginia Tech, Lynn currently coordinates public affairs for the College of Forestry and Wildlife Resources and the Virginia Sea Grant College Program. She has won numerous top national awards for her publications at the University of Maryland, Hollins College, and the Roanoke Valley Regional Chamber of Commerce. When she coached field hockey at Roanoke's North Cross School, Lynn discovered tidbits she did not already know about the state while looking for teams to play. She has also worked for the National Park Service's Blue Ridge Parkway and currently serves as vice president of Friends of the Blue Ridge Parkway board. For her work to preserve parkway viewsheds from over-development, she received the Garden Club of Virginia's Dugdale Award for Conservation in 1995. She is president of Roanoke's Valley Beautiful and serves on the Virginia Museum of Natural History's Foundation board. A lifelong learner and lover of history whose book and archival collections are running her family out of home, Lynn has always admired Robert E. Lee, the consummate leader with integrity; she is pictured here in Roanoke along the Lee Highway named in honor of the great general.

Bruce W. Muncy, a native of Dayton, Ohio, studied at Wright State University and received a commercial photography degree from the Ohio Institute of Photography in Dayton. His photography business in Roanoke, Virginia, specializes in architectural photography, product illustration, and business portraits. Bruce's work has appeared in "Bed & Breakfast Guide (Southeast)" and in numerous magazines including *National Geographic Traveler, Country Inns,* and *Innsider.* He has taught at the Winona School of International Photography in Chicago, Illinois; the Georgia School of Photography in Helen, Georgia; and the Ohio Institute of Photography in Dayton. Bruce won Virginia's highest photographic award, the *Kodak Award of Excellence,* two consecutive years and was awarded the degrees of *Master of Photography* and *Photographic Craftsman* by the Professional Photographers of America. When not "shooting" for his books, the single parent enjoys hiking, cycling, and traveling with his children, Brian and Sara. He even likes taking a busman's holiday — for him that's photographing for pleasure. A gourmet cook to boot, he can vouch that Virginia's innkeepers know how to prepare food.

DIRECTORY TO B & B's, INNS & RSO's

*Alphabetized by city: There are many fine establishments listed here, some known to us but many we have not visited. We encourage you to write for information and talk with the innkeepers to be sure their facilities meet your needs and expectations. * Denotes members of the Bed & Breakfast Assoc. of Virginia.* **Boldface** *denotes featured B&B's and Inns.*

ABINGDON
Maplewood Farm B&B *
RR 7 Box 461
Abingdon, VA   24210-8846
540-628-2640

Summerfield Inn *
101 Valley St
Abingdon, VA   24210-2811
540-628-5905

Victoria & Albert Inn
224 Oak Hill St NE
Abingdon, VA   24210-2824
540-678-2797

Martha Washington Inn
PO Box 1037
Abingdon, VA   24210-1037
540-628-3161

Maxwell Manor
19215 Old Jonesboro Rd
Abingdon, VA 24210
540-628-3912

Lone Willow Inn
247 Valley St NE
Abingdon, VA   24210-2909

Cabin on the River *
146 Crestview Dr NE
Abingdon, VA   24210-2010
540-628-8433

Silversmith Inn *
102 E Main St
Abingdon, VA   24210-2808
540-676-3924

Inn on Town Creek *
PO Box 1745
Abingdon, VA   24210-1349
540-628-4560

AFTON
Starcrest B&B
RR 2 Box 470
Afton, VA   22920-9449
540-361-2335

Afton House
PO Box 46
Afton, VA   22920-0046
540-456-6759

Looking Glass House *
RR 3 Box 183
Afton, VA   22920-9407
540-456-6844

ALBERTA
Englewood B&B *
RR 1 Box 141
Alberta, VA   23821-9743

ALDIE
Little River Inn
PO Box 116
Aldie, VA   22001-0116
703-327-6742

ALEXANDRIA
Princely B&B Ltd
819 Prince St
Alexandria, VA   22314-3006
703-683-2159

ALTAVISTA
Castle to Country House
1010 Main St
Altavista, VA   24517-1531
804-369-4911

AMHERST
Dulwich Manor *
RR 5 Box 173A
Amherst, VA   24521-9060
804-946-7207

Rutledge Inn
PO Box 890
Amherst, VA   24521-0890

Fairview B&B *
RR 4 Box 117
Amherst, VA   24521-9216
804-277-8500

AMISSVILLE
Bunree
Amissville, VA   22002
703-937-4133

ARLINGTON
Memory House *
6404 Washington Blvd
Arlington, VA   22205-1954
703-534-4607

Crystal B&B
2620 S Fern St
Arlington, VA   22202-2512

Oak Grove Plantation B&B
3316 21st Ave N
Arlington, VA   22207-3821

ASHLAND
Henry Clay Inn *
PO Box 135
Ashland, VA   23005-0135
804-798-3100

Wisteria Inn
303 Maple St
Ashland, VA   23005-2121
804-798-9494

BASSETT
Annie's Country Inn
RR 5 Box 562
Bassett, VA   24055-9201

BATESVILLE
Westbury
PO Box 91
Batesville, VA   22924-0091

BEDFORD
Bedford House
422 Avenel Ave
Bedford, VA   24523-1916
540-586-5050

Elmo's Rest Farm House
RR 2 Box 198
Bedford, VA   24523-9638
540-586-3707

Otter's Den
RR 2 Box 160E
Bedford, VA   24523-9629

Peaks of Otter Lodge
PO Box 489
Bedford, VA   24523-0489
540-586-1081

BENTONVILLE
Statewood Bed & Breakfast
RR 1 Box 242
Bentonville, VA   22610-9734
703-635-9070

Creekside B&B
Rt 649
Bentonville, VA   22610

BERRYVILLE
Blue Ridge B&B
RR 2 Box 3895
Berryville, VA   22611-9527
540-955-1246

Battletown Inn
102 West Main St
Berryville, VA   22611
540-955-4100

BLACKSBURG
L'Arche Farm B & B *
1867 Tabor Rd
Blacksburg, VA   24060
540-951-1808

Sycamore Tree B&B *
PO Box 10937
Blacksburg, VA   24062-0937
540-381-1597

Clay Corner Inn *
401 Clay St SW
Blacksburg, VA   24060-4708
540-953-2604

Brush Mountain Inn *
3030 Mt Tabor Rd
Blacksburg, VA   24062
540-951-7530

Twin Porches B&B *
318 Clay St SW
Blacksburg, VA   24060
540-552-0930

BLACKSTONE
Epes House B&B *
210 College Avenue
Blackstone, VA 23824
804-292-7941

BLAND
Willow Bend Farm B&B *
RR 1 Box 235
Bland, VA   24315-9750
540-688-3719

BLUEGRASS
Bluegrass B&B
General Delivery
Blue Grass, VA   24413-9999

BOSTON
Thistle Hill B&B *
RR 1 Box 291
Boston, VA   22713-9610
540-987-9142

BOWLING GREEN
Mansion View Bed & Breakfast *
PO Box 787
Bowling Green, VA   22427
804-633-4377

BOYCE
River House *
RR 2 Box 135
Boyce, VA   22620-9611
540-837-1476

BRANDY STATION
Blue Haven B&B *
14648 Carrico Mills Rd
Brandy Station, VA 22714
540-825-0716

BRIDGEWATER
Bear & Dragon B&B
401 N Main St
Bridgewater, VA   22812-1622

BRISTOL
Glencarin Manor
224 Old Abingdon Hwy.
Bristol, VA 24201
540-466-0224

BROADWAY
Loomis Stable Inn
RR 2 Box 186H
Broadway, VA   22815-9313

Susie Q Farm B&B
RR 3 Box 82A
Broadway, VA   22815-9149

BRODNAX
Sherwood Manor Inn/Restaurant
RR 2 Box 270
Brodnax, VA   23920-9337
804-848-0361

BROOKNEAL
Stauton Hill *
RR 2, Box 244B
Brookneal, VA 24528
804-376-4048

BUMPASS
Rockland Farm Retreat
3609 Lewiston Rd
Bumpass, VA   23024-9659

BURKES GARDEN
James Burke Inn
PO Box 462
Burkes Garden, VA   24608-0462
703-472-2114

CAPE CHARLES
Sea Gate, A Bed & Breakfast
9 Tazewell Ave
Cape Charles, VA   23310-1345
804-331-2206

B&B of Pickett's Harbor
RR 1 Box 97AA
Cape Charles, VA   23310
804-331-2212

Cape Charles House
645 Tazwell Ave
Cape Charles, VA   23310
804-331-4920

Chesapeake Charm B&B
202 Madison Avenue
Cape Charles, VA 23310
804-331-2676

Nottingham Ridge B&B
RR 1 Box 97B
Cape Charles, VA   23310-9719
804-331-1010

Sunset Inn B&B
108 Bay Avenue
Cape Charles, VA 23310
804-331-2424

CAPRON
Sandy Hill Farm B&B
RR 1 Box 55
Capron, VA   23829-9720

CASTLETON
Blue Knoll Farm
RR 1 Box 141
Castleton, VA   22716-9736
540-937-5234

CATAWABA
Crosstrail B&B
5880 Blacksburg Rd.
Catawba, VA 24070
540-384-8078

CHAMPLAIN
Linden House
Tidewater Tr., Rt. 17
Champlain, VA 22438
800-662-1202

CHARLES CITY
North Bend Plantation B&B *
12200 Weyanoke Rd
Charles City, VA 23030-3632
804-829-5176

Piney Grove at Southall's
Plantation
16920 Southall Plantation Ln
Charles City, VA   23030-9735
804-829-2480

Edgewood Plantation
RR 2 Box 490
Charles City, VA   23030-9617
804-829-2962

Belle Air Plantation
11800 John Tyler Memor Hwy
Charles City, VA   23030-3614

Country Antique
10111 John Tyler Memor Hwy
Charles City, VA   23030-3402

CHARLOTTESVILLE
Clifton Country Inn
RR 13 Box 26
Charlottesville, VA   22901-7927
804-971-1800

Inn at Sugar Hollow Farm *
P.O. box 5705
Charlottesville, VA 22905
804-823-2002

Silver Thatch Inn *
3001 Hollymead Dr
Charlottesville, VA   22901-7422
804-978-4686

Guesthouses B&B Inc
PO Box 5737
Charlottesville, VA   22905-5737
804-979-7264

200 South Street Inn
200 W South St
Charlottesville, VA   22902
804-979-0200

The Quarters *
611 Preston Ave
Charlottesville, VA 22903
804-979-7264

The 1817 Historic B&B *
1211 W. Main St
Charlottesville, VA 22903
804-979-7353

CHATHAM
Eldon - The Inn at Chatham
RR 1, Box 254B (SR 685)
Chatham, VA 24531
804-432-0935

House of Laird B&B
P.O. Box 1131
Chatham, VA 24531
804-432-2523

Sims Mitchel House
242 Whittle St.
Chatham, VA 24531
804-432-0595

CHESTERFIELD
Bellmont Manor B&B *
6600 Bellmont Rd.
Chesterfield, VA 23832
804-745-0106

CHILLHOWIE
Clarkcrest B&B *
Star Route Box 60
Chillhowie, VA 24319
540-646-3707

Pendleton House Inn *
144 Sulphur Springs Rd
Chilhowie, Va 24319
540-646-2047

CHINCOTEAGUE
Year of the Horse Inn
600 Main St S
Chincoteague, VA   23336

Island manor House *
4160 Main St
Chincoteague, VA   23336
804-336-5436

Miss molly's Inn *
4141Main St
Chincoteague, VA 23336
804-336-6686

Watson House B&B *
4240 Main St
Chincoteague, VA   23336
804-336-1564

Channel Bass Inn
100 Church Street
Chincoteague, VA 23336
804-336-6148

CHRISTIANSBURG
Evergreen *
The Belle-Caozzi House
201 E. Main St.
Christiansburg, VA 24073
540-382-7372

Oaks Victorian Inn
311 E. Main St
Christiansburg, VA 24073
540-381-1500

CHURCHVILLE
Buckhorn Inn
HC 33 Box 139
Churchville, VA   24421
540-357-6900

CLARKSVILLE
Needmoor Inn *
PO Box 629
Clarksville, VA   23927-0629
804-374-2866

Noreen's Nest *
PO Box 356
Clarksville, VA   23927-0356
804-374-0603

Kinderton Manor Inn
RR 1 Box 19A
Clarksville, VA 23927

CLUSTER SPRINGS
Oak Grove Plantation B&B *
PO Box 45
Cluster Springs, VA   24535
804-575-7137

CLIFTON FORGE
Longdale Inn *
6209 Longdale Furnance Rd.
Clifton Forge, VA 24422
540-862-0892

COLUMBIA
Upper Byrd Farm B&B *
6452 River Rd W
Columbia, VA   23038-2002
804-842-2240

COVINGTON
Milton Hall B&B *
207 Thorny Ln
Covington, VA   24426-9803
540-965-0196

CROZET
Buxton Sugar Hollow
RR 2 Box 350
Crozet, VA   22932-9636

Rivendell
RR 1 Box 619
Crozet, VA   22932-9743

CULPEPER
Fountain Hall B&B *
609 S East St
Culpeper, VA   22701-3222
540-825-8200

DANVILLE
Dula-Penn House
1031 Main St
Danville, VA 24541
804-797-3088

Broad Street Manor
124 Broad St
Danville, VA 24541

Gold Leaf Inn *
1012 Main St
Danville, VA 24541
804-793-1433

DAVIS WHARF
Bay View B&B
35350 Copes Dr
Davis Wharf, VA 23345
804-442-6963

DELTAVILLE
River's Rise B&B *
P.O. Box 18
Hardyville, VA 23070
804-776-7521

DILLWYN
Tranquility Farm B&B
RR 3 Box 174
Dillwyn, VA 23936
804-393-4456

DRAPER
Claytor Lake Homestead Inn
P.O. Box 7
Draper, Va 24324
540-980-6777

DUBLIN
Bell's B&B *
PO Box 405
Dublin, VA 24084-0405
540-674-6331

EDINBURG
Mary's Country Inn
RR 2 Box 4
Edinburg, VA 22824-9501
540-984-8286

ELKTON
Joannes's B&B
RR 2 Box 276
Elkton, VA 22827-9634
540-298-9723

ETLAN
Dulaney Hollow @ Old Rag Mtn.
HC 2 Box 215
Etlan, VA 22727-9301
540-923-4470

EXMORE
Martha's Inn *
12224 Lincoln Ave
Exmore, VA 23350
804-442-4641

FAIRFAX
Bailiwick Inn
4023 Chain Bridge Rd
Fairfax, VA 22030-4101
703-691-2266

FANCY GAP
Cascades Mountain Inn
RR 2
Fancy Gap, VA 24328-9802

FARMVILLE
Lanscott House
408 High St
Farmville, VA 23901-1812

FINCASTLE
Fincastle Gallery
110 Roanoke St
Fincastle, VA 24090
540-473-2974

FLINT HILL
Caledonia Farm B & B *
RR 1 Box 2080
Flint Hill, VA 22627-9803
540-675-3693

Stone House Hollow
RR 1 Box 20901
Flint Hill, VA 22627-9803
540-675-3279

FLOYD
Brookfield Inn
PO Box 341
Floyd, VA 24091-0341

FOREST
Summer Kitchen
RR 4 Box 538
Forest, VA 24551
804-525-0923

FRANKTOWN
Stillmeadow Inn
PO Box 144
Franktown, VA 23354-0144
804-442-2431

Walker's Inn
PO Box 14
Franktown, VA 23354-0014

FREDERICKSBURG
Fredericksburg Colonial Inn
1707 Princess Anne St
Fredericksburg, VA 22401-3524

La Vista Plantation *
4420 Guinea Station Rd
Fredericksburg, VA 22408-8850
540-898-8444

Richard Johnston Inn
711 Caroline St
Fredericksburg, VA 22401

Smith Cottage
303 Fauquier St
Fredericksburg, VA 22401-3713

McGrath House
225 Princess Ann St
Fredericksburg, VA 22401-6046

Spooner House B&B, The
1300 Caroline St
Fredericksburg, VA 22401-3704
540-371-1267

Mary Josephine Ball B&B *
1203 Prince Edward St
Fredericksburg, VA 22401
540-373-7674

FRONT ROYAL
Chester House Inn *
43 Chester St
Front Royal, VA 22630-3368
540-635-3937

Constant Spring Inn
413 S Royal Ave
Front Royal, VA 22630-3229
540-635-7010

Killahevlin *
1401 N Royal Ave
Front Royal, VA 22630-3625
540-636-7335

GLOUCESTER
Airville Plantation *
RR 3 Box 1193
Gloucester, VA 23061-9121
804-693-3084

The Willows B&B *
5344 Roanes Wharf Rd
Gloucester, VA 23061
804-693-4066

GORDONSVILLE
Norfields Farm B&B *
RR 1 Box 477
Gordonsville, VA 22942
540-832-5939

Sleepy Hollow Farm *
16280 Blue Ridge Tpke
Gordonsville, VA 22942
540-832-5555

Rocklands B&B
17439 Rocklands Dr
Gordonsville, VA 22942
540-832-7176

GORE
Rainbow's End
RR 1 Box 335
Gore, VA 22637-9729

GOSHEN
Hummingbird Inn *
P.O. Box 147
Goshen, VA 24439
540-997-9065

GREENWOOD
Longhouse
RR 1 Box 278
Greenwood, VA 22943

HAMILTON
Stonegate B&B
325 W Colonial Hwy
Hamilton, VA 22068-9002
703-338-9519

HARRISONBURG
Joshua Wilton House *
412 S Main St
Harrisonburg, VA 22801
540-434-4464

Kingsway B&B
3581 Singers Glen Rd
Harrisonburg, VA 22801-8310
540-867-9696

HILLSBORO
Inn Between the Hills
RR 9 Box
Hillsboro, VA 22132

HILLSVILLE
Bray's Manor B&B Inn *
RR 3 Box 210
Hillsville, VA 24343-8305
540-728-7901

HINTON
Boxwood Inn
RR 1 Box 130
Hinton, VA 22831-9712

HOT SPRINGS
King's Victorian Inn *
RR 2 Box 622
Hot Springs, VA 24445-9614
540-839-3134

Carriage Court
RR 2 Box 620
Hot Springs, VA 24445

Vine Cottage Inn
PO Box 918
Hot Springs, VA 24445
540-839-2422

HOWARDSVILLE
Fish Pond Plantation
RR 1 Box 48
Howardsville, VA 24562-9705

HUNTLY
Windsor Lodge
Rt 522
Huntly, VA 22640

INDEPENDENCE
River View B&B *
PO Box 686
Independence, VA 24348
540-236-4187

IRVINGTON
King Carter Inn
PO Box 425
Irvington, VA 22480-0425

LANCASTER
Inn at Levelfields
P.O. Box 216
Lancaster, VA 22503

LAWRENCEVILLE
Sherwood Manor Inn
Rt 2, Box 268
Lawrenceville, VA 23920
804-848-0361

LEESBURG
Cornerstone B&B *
16882 Clarks Gap Rd
Paeonian Springs,VA 22129
703-882-3722

Fleetwood Farm B&B *
RR 1 Box 306A
Leesburg, VA 22075-8716
703-327-4325

Green Tree
15 S King St
Leesburg, VA 22075-2903

Colonial Inn of Leesburg
19 S King St
Leesburg, VA 22075-2903

Norris House Inn *
108 Loudoun St SW
Leesburg, VA 22075-2909
703-777-1806

Laurel Brigade Inn
20 W Market St
Leesburg, VA 22075-2805
703-777-1010

LEXINGTON
Lavendar Hill Farm B&B Inn *
RR 1, Box 515 (SR 631)
Lexington, VA 24450
800-446-4240

Llewellyn Lodge at Lexington *
603 S Main St
Lexington, VA 24450-2245
540-463-3235

Seven Hills Inn
408 S Main St
Lexington, VA 24450-2346
540-463-4715

Historic Country Inns
11 N Main St
Lexington, VA 24450-2520
540-463-2044

Fassifern B&B *
RR 5 Box 87
Lexington, VA 24450-8816
540-463-1013

Maple Hall
11 N Main St
Lexington, VA 24450-2520
540-463-2044

McCampbell Inn
11 N Main St
Lexington, VA 24450-2520
540-463-2044

Alexander-Withrow House
3 W Washington St
Lexington, VA 24450-2120
540-463-2044

Wayland's Guest House
206 W Washington St
Lexington, VA 24450-2116

Inn at Union Run
RR 3 Box 68
Lexington, VA 24450
540-463-9715

LINCOLN
Springdale Country Inn
RR 2 Box 356
Lincoln, VA 22078
703-338-1832

Oakland Green B&B
PO Box 154
Lincoln, VA 22078-0154
703-338-7628

Creek Crossing Farm B&B
PO Box 18
Lincoln, VA 22078-0018
703-338-7550

LOCUST DALE
Inn at Meander Plantation *
HC 5 Box 460
Locust Dale, VA 22948
800-383-4936

LOCUSTVILLE
Wynne Tref
PO Box 96
Locustville, VA 23404-0096
804-787-2356

LOUISA
Sleepytown B&B
PO Box 1609
Louisa, VA 23093-1609

Ginger Hill B&B
RR 5 Box 33E
Louisa, VA 23093-8913
540-967-0589

LOUISA TOWN
Whistle Stop B&B *
318 Main St
Lousia Town, VA 23093
540-967-2911

LOWESVILLE
Fairview B&B *
RR 4 Box 117
Amherst, VA 24521
804-277-8500

LURAY
Mountain View House
151 S. Court Street
Luray, VA 22835
540-743-3723

Ruffner House
P.O. Box 620, Box 4
Luray, VA 22835
540-743-7855

Shenandoah River Roost
Rt. 3, Box 224-B
Luray, VA 22835
540-743-3467

Woodruff House *
330 Mechanic St
Luray, VA 22835
540-743-1494

LYNCHBURG
Langhorne Manor *
313 Washington St
Lynchburg, VA 24504-4619
804-846-4667

Lynchburg Mansion Inn B&B *
405 Madison St
Lynchburg, VA 24504-2455
804-528-5400

Madison House B&B *
413 Madison St
Lynchburg, VA 24504-2435
804-528-1503

Sojourners Bed & Breakfast
PO Box 3587
Lynchburg, VA 24503-0587

Ivanhoe
RR 3 Box 266
Lynchburg, VA 24504-9753
804-332-7103

Once Upon A Time
1102 Harrison St
Lynchburg, VA 24504
804-845-3561

LYNDHURST
Cabin Creekwood
RR 1 Box 402
Lyndhurst, VA 22952-9601

A Mountain Place
RR 1 Box 425
Lyndhurst, VA 22952-9602
703-943-7203

MADISON *
Shenandoah Spgs Country Inn
HC 6 Box 122
Madison, VA 22722-9606
540-923-4300

MADISON HEIGHTS
Winridge B&B *
RR 1 Box 362
Madison Heights, VA 24572
804-384-7220

MANASSAS
Bennett House B&B *
9252 Bennett Dr
Manassass, VA 22110
703-368-6121

Sunrise Hill Farm B&B *
5513 Sudley Rd
Manassas, VA 22110-2104
703-754-8309

MATHEWS
Ravenswood Inn
PO Box 250
Mathews, VA 23109-0250
804-725-7272

MC GAHEYSVILLE
Shenandoah Valley Farm & Inn
RR 1 Box 142
Mc Gaheysville, VA 22840-9732

MEADOWS OF DAN
Spangler's B&B
RR 2
Meadows of Dan, VA 24120-9802

MIDDLEBURG
Chase's
US Hwy 50
Middleburg, VA 22117
540-592-3680

Poor House Farm B&B *
35304 Poor House Lane
Round Hill, VA 22141
540-554-2511

Red Fox Inn & Mosby's Tavern
PO Box 385
Middleburg, VA 22117-0385
540-687-6301

Briar Patch at Middleburg
PO Box 803
Middleburg, VA 22117-0803

Welbourne
RR 1 Box 300
Middleburg, VA 22117-9102
540-687-3201

McConnell House
PO Box 385
Middleburg, VA 22117-0385

Middleburg Country Inn
PO Box 2065
Middleburg, VA 22117-2065
540-687-6082

Middleburg Inn & Guest Suites
PO Box 984
Middleburg, VA 22117
540-687-3115

MIDDLETOWN
Main Street B&B
8004 Main St
Middletown, VA 22645-9529
703-869-5309

Wayside Inn
7783 Main Street, Rt 11
Middletown, VA 22645
703-869-1797

MILLBORO
Nimrod Hall
HC 4 Box 31
Millboro, VA   24460-9607

Fort Lewis Lodge
RR 1 Box 21A
Millboro, VA   24460-9507
540-925-2314

MILLWOOD
Brookside *
Millwood, VA   22646
703-837-1780

MINERAL
Littlepage Inn *
15701 Monrovia Rd
Mineral, VA   23117
540-854-9861

MOLLUSK
Greenvale Manor Inn *
PO Box 70
Mollusk, VA   22517-0070
804-462-5995

MONETA
Holland-Duncan House
RR 5 Box 681
Moneta, VA   24121-9464
540-721-8510

MONROE
St Moor House *
RR 1 Box 136
Monroe, VA   24574-9724
804-929-8228

MONTEREY
Bobbie's B&B
HC 2 Box 5
Monterey, VA   24465-9401
540-468-2308

Highland Inn
PO Box 40
Monterey, VA   24465-0040
540-468-2143

Cherry Hill
PO Box 220
Monterey, VA   24465-0220
540-468-2972

MONTROSS
Inn at Montross
PO Box 908
Montross, VA   22520-0908
804-493-9097

Pearson House
RR 3
Montross, VA   22520-9803

MORATTICO
Holly Point
PO Box 64
Morattico, VA   22523-0064

MOUNT CRAWFORD
Pumpkin House Inn
RR 2 Box 155
Mount Crawford, VA   22841
540-434-6903

MOUNT HOLLY
Mount Holly Steamboat Inn
PO Box 130
Mount Holly, VA   22524-0130
804-472-3336

MOUNT JACKSON
Widow Kip's Country Inn *
RR 1 Box 117
Mount Jackson, VA   22842-9742
540-477-2400

Sky Chalet
PO Box 28
Mount Jackson, VA   22842-0028

MOUNT SIDNEY
Spiff Inn
RR 1 Box 8
Mount Sidney, VA   24467-9705
540-248-7307

MOUNT SOLON
Short Glade Farm
RR 1 Box 99
Mount Solon, VA   22843-9718

NATURAL BRIDGE
Burger's Country Inn *
RR 2 Box 564
Natural Bridge, VA   24578-9616
540-291-2464

NELLYSFORD
Meander Inn *
PO Box 443
Nellysford, VA   22958-0443
804-361-1121

The Mark Addy *
RR 1 Box 375
Nellysford, VA   22958-9526
804-361-1101

Trillium House *
PO Box 280
Nellysford, VA   22958-0280
804-325-9126

Acorn Inn
PO Box 431
Nellysford, VA   22958-0431
804-361-9357

NEW CHURCH
Garden & The Sea Inn *
PO Box 275
New Church, VA   23415-0275
804-824-0672

NEW MARKET
Red Shutter Farmhouse B&B *
RR 1 Box 376
New Market, VA   22844-9306
540-740-4281

Touch of Country B&B
9329 N Congress St
New Market, VA   22844-9508
540-740-8030

NEWPORT
Newport House
RR 2 Box 561E
Newport, VA   24128-9560

NORFOLK
Page House Inn *
323 Fairfax Ave
Norfolk, VA   23507-2215
757-625-5033

Bed & Breakfast of Tidewater *
PO Box 6226
Norfolk, VA   23514-0001
757-627-1983

Cameron Residence
1605 Bill St
Norfolk, VA   23518-5901

B&B Larchmont
1112 Buckingham Ave
Norfolk, VA   23508-1513

Ericka's B&B
232 E Bayview Blvd
Norfolk, VA   23503-5249

B&B of Tidewater
PO Box 6226
Norfolk, VA   23508-0226

NORTH
Cedar Point Country Inn
PO Box 369
North, VA   23128-0369

NORTH GARDEN
Inn At The Crossroads *
RR 2 Box 6
North Garden, VA   22959-9702
804-979-6452

Ingleside Farm
RR 1 Box 372
North Garden, VA   22959-9614

Clover Green Farm
RR 2 Box 36
North Garden, VA 22959

ONANCOCK
Colonial Manor Inn
PO Box 94
Onancock, VA   23417-0094
804-787-3521

The Spinning Wheel
31 North Street
Onancock, Va 23417
804-787-7311

ORANGE
Hidden Inn
249 Caroline St
Orange, VA   22960-1529
540-672-3625

Holladay House *
155 W Main St
Orange, VA   22960-1528
540-672-4893

Shadows Bed & Breakfast Inn
RR 1 Box 535
Orange, VA   22960-9737
540-672-5057

Willow Grove Inn *
9478 James Madison Hwy
Orange, VA   22960-9706
540-672-5982

ORLEANS
Hilltop Manor
PO Box 36
Orlean, VA   22128-0036

OYSTER
Penland Inn
SR 600
Oyster, VA   23419

PAEONIAN SPRING
Cornerstone B&B *
RR 1 Box 82C
Paeonian Spring, VA   22129

PALMYRA
Palmer Country Manor *
RR 2 Box 1390
Palmyra, VA   22963-9414
804-589-1300

Danscot House Bed & Breakfast *
PO Box 157
Palmyra, VA   22963-0157
804-589-1977

PARIS
Ashby Inn
RR 1 Box 2A
Paris, VA   22130-9004
540-592-3900

PETERSBURG
High Street Inn *
405 W High St
Petersburg, VA   23803-3857
804-733-0505

Mayfield Inn
PO Box 2265
Petersburg, VA   23804-1565
804-733-0866

Folly Castle Inn B&B
323 W. Washington At
Petersburg, VA 23803
804-733-6463

PHILOMONT
Dandongreen Manor B&B
P.O. Box 194
Philomont, VA 22131-0194
703-338-4202

POCAHONTAS
Laurel Inn
100 W Water St
Pocahontas, VA   24635

PORT HAYWOOD
Inn at Tabb's Creek Landing *
PO Box 219
Port Haywood, VA   23138
804-725-5136

PORT REPUBLIC
Busy Bee B&B
RR 1 Box 813
Port Republic, VA   24471-9746
540-289-5480

PORTSMOUTH
Olde Towne Inn *
420 Middle St
Portsmouth, VA 23704
757-397-5462

POUNDING MILL
Cuz's Cabins and Resort
US Route 460
Pounding Mill, VA 24637
540-964-9014

PRATTS
Colvin Hall *
HC 3 Box 30g
Pratts, VA 22731
703-948-6211

PROVIDENCE FORGE
Jasmine Plantation B&B *
4500 N. Courthouse Rd
Providence Forge, VA 23140
804-966-9836

PUNGOTEAGUE
Evergreen Inn *
PO Box 102
Pungoteague, VA   23422-0102
804-442-3375

PULASKI
Count Pulaski B&B *
821 N. Jefferson Ave
Pulaski, VA 24301
540-980-1163

PURCELLVILLE
The Cottage
511 S. 32nd St, Rt 690
Purcellville, VA 22132
703-338-3225

RADFORD
Alleghany Inn *
1123 Grove Ave
Radford, Va 24141
540-731-4466

RAPHINE
Oak Skpring Farm & Vineyard *
RR 1 Box 356
Raphine, VA 24472
540-377-2398

REEDVILLE
Cedar Grove B&B *
PO Box 2535
Reedville, VA   22539
804-453-3915

Elizabeth House B&B *
PO Box 163
Reedville, VA   22539-0163
804-453-7016

RICHMOND
Abbie Hill Guest Lodging *
PO Box 4503
Richmond, VA   23220-8503
804-335-5855

Be My Guest B&B
2926 Kensington Ave
Richmond, VA   23221-2419
804-358-9901

Emmanuel Hutzler House *
2036 Monument Ave
Richmond, VA   23220-2708
804-353-6900

Mr Patrick Henry's Inn *
2300 E Broad St
Richmond, VA   23223-7061
804-644-1322

West Bocock House *
1107 Grove Ave
Richmond, VA   23220-4706
804-358-6174

Carrington Row Inn
2309 E Broad St
Richmond, VA   23223-7126
804-343-7005

William Catlin House B&B *
2304 E Broad St
Richmond, VA   23223-7127
804-780-3746

RIVERTON
Dellbrook Manor
PO Box 221
Riverton, VA   22651

ROANOKE
Mary Bladon House *
381 Washington Ave SW
Roanoke, VA   24016-4303
540-344-5361

Country Inn
6910 Williamson Rd
Roanoke, VA   24019-4229
540-366-1987

B&B of Roanoke Valley
1708 Arlington Rd SW
Roanoke, VA   24015-2806
540-344-5620

ROCKY MOUNT
Claiborne House *
115 Claiborne Ave
Rocky Mount, VA   24151-1412
540-483-4616

Amber Inn
RR 2 Box 181A
Rocky Mount, VA   24151

ROUND HILL
Poor House Farm B&B
RR 1 Box 218
Round Hill, VA   22141-9107
540-554-2511

SALEM
Old Manse B&B
530 E Main St
Salem, VA   24153-4319
540-389-3921

Nathaniel Burwell House
530 E Main St
Salem, VA   24153-4319
540-389-3921

Inn at Burwell Place
601 W Main St
Salem, VA   24153-3515
540-387-0250

SCOTTSVILLE
Chester B&B
243 James River Rd
Scottsville, VA   24590-9713
804-286-3960

High Meadows Vineyard and
Mountain Sunset Inn *
RR 4 Box 6
Scottsville, VA   24590-9706
804-286-2218

SMITHFIELD
Smithfield Station
415 S. Church St
Smithfield, VA 23430
757-357-7700

SPERRYVILLE
Conyers House & Stable
RR 1 Box 157
Sperryville, VA   22740-9729
540-987-8025

Nether's Mill
RR 1 Box 62
Sperryville, VA   22740-9614
540-987-8625

Apple Hill Farm
Sperryville, VA   22740
540-987-9454

SPOTSYLVANIA
Rocksbury Mill
6908 Roxbury Mill Rd
Spotsylvania, VA   22553-2438
540-582-6611

Roxbury Mill *
6908 Roxbury Mill Rd
Spotsylvania, VA   22553-2438
540-582-6611

SPRINGFIELD
Bonnie Mill B&B
7305 Bonniemill Ln
Springfield, VA   22150-4404

STAFFORD
Renaissance Manor
2247 Courthouse Road
Stafford, VA 22554
540-720-3785

STANDARDSVILLE
Edgewood Farm B&B *
RR 2 Box 303
Stanardsville, VA   22973-9405
804-985-3782

STANLEY
Milton House
PO Box 366
Stanley, VA   22851-0366
540-778-3451

Jordan Hollow Farm Inn
RR 2 Box 375
Stanley, VA   22851-9538
540-778-2285

STAUNTON
Frederick House *
P.O. Box 1387
Staunton, VA 24401
540-885-4220

Kenwood *
235 E. Beverley St
Staunton, VA 24401
540-885-7026

Thornrose House *
531 Thornrose Ave
Staunton, VA   24401-3161
540-885-7026

Bellefonte
1610 New Hope
Stauton, VA 24401
540-886-7530

Belle Grae Inn
515 W Frederick St
Staunton, VA   24401-3333
540-886-5151

Ashton Country House *
1205 Middlebrook Ave
Staunton, VA   24401-4546
540-885-7819

Sampson Eagon Inn *
238 E Beverley St
Staunton, VA   24401-4325
540-886-8200

STEELES TAVERN
Osceola Mill Country Inn
Rt 56
Steeles Tavern, VA   24476
540-377-6455

**Steeles Tavern Manor *
P.O. Box 39, HWY 11
Steeles Tavern, VA 24476
800-743-8666**

STRASBURG
Vesper Hall
PO Box 575
Strasburg, VA   22657-0575

Tumbling Run B&B
RR 1 Box 11
Strasburg, VA   22657-9705
540-465-3226

Eberly House B&B
214 W Washington St
Strasburg, VA   22657-1452
540-465-3226

STUARTS DRAFT
Oak Lawn B&B
RR 4 Box 405
Stuarts Draft, VA   24477-9736
540-337-4145

SURRY
Seward House Inn *
PO Box 352
Surry, VA   23883-0352
757-294-3810

SWOOPE
Lambsgate B&B *
RR 1 Box 63
Swoope, VA   24479-9709
540-337-6929

SYRIA
Graves Mountain Lodge
RT 670
Syria, VA 22743
703-923-4231

TANGIER
Sunset Inn
PO Box 156
Tangier, VA   23440-0156

TOWNSEND
Pickett's Harbor
PO Box 96
Townsend, VA   23443-0096
804-331-2212

TREVILIANS
**Prospect Hill
RR 3 Box 430
Trevilians, VA   23093-9314
800-277-0844**

TROUTDALE
Fox Hill Inn *
RR 2 Box 11
Troutdale, VA   24378-9501
540-677-3313

TROUTVILLE
Woods Edge
RR 2 Box 645
Troutville, VA   24175-9591

UPPERVILLE
1763 Inn
RR 1 Box 19D
Upperville, VA   22176-9702
703-592-3848

URBANNA
Duck Farm Inn
PO Box 787
Urbanna, VA   23175-0787
804-758-5685

Town House
1880 Prince George St
Urbanna, VA   23175

Atherston Hall B&B P
250 Prince George St
Urbanna, VA   23175
804-758-2809

VESUVIUS
Irish Gap Inns *
RR 1 Box 40
Vesuvius, VA   24483-9401
804-922-7701

VIRGINIA BEACH
Angie's Guest Cottage *
302 24th St
Virginia Beach, VA   23451-3221
757-428-4690

**Church Point Manor
4001 Church Point Rd
Virginia Beach, VA 23455
757-460-2657**

Picket Fence
209 43rd St
Virginia Beach, VA   23451-2503

Barclay Cottage *
400 16th St
Virginia Beach, VA   23451-3406
757-422-1956

WACHAPREAGUE
Burton House
PO Box 182
Wachapreague, VA   23480-0182
804-787-4560

WARM SPRINGS
**Anderson Cottage *
PO Box 176
Warm Springs, VA   24484
540-839-2975**

Warm Springs Inn
PO Box 27
Warm Springs, VA   24484-0027
540-839-5351

**Inn at Gristmill Square
PO Box 359
Warm Springs, VA   24484-0359
540-839-2231**

Three Hills Inn
PO Box 99
Warm Springs, VA   24484-0099
540-839-5381

**Meadow Lane Lodge
HC 1 Box 110A
Warm Springs, VA   24484
540-839-5959**

WARRENTON
The Black Horse Inn
8393 Meetze Rd
Warrenton, VA 22186
540-349-4020

Rosemont Farm Inn
RR 3 Box 240
Warrenton, VA   22186-8908

WARSAW
Greenwood
RR 2 Box 50
Warsaw, VA   22572

WASHINGTON
Heritage House *
PO Box 427
Washington, VA   22747-0427
540-675-3207

**Sycamore Hill House &
Gardens *
RR 1 Box 978
Washington, VA   22747-9737
540-675-3046**

Inn at Little Washington
P.O. Box 300
Washington, VA 22747

Gay Street Inn
P.O. box 237
Washington, VA 22747
540-675-3288

Foster-Harris House
P.O. box 333
Washington, VA 22747

Blue Rock Inn
RR 1 Box 555
Washington, VA 22747
540-987-3190

WATERFORD
Pink House B&B
116 Main St
Waterford, VA 22190
703-882-3453

James Moore House
P.O. Box 227
Waterford, VA 22190

Waterford Inn
PO Box 227
Waterford, VA   22190-0227

WAYNESBORO
Meadow Run B&B
RR 2 Box 308
Waynesboro, VA   22980-9549
540-943-6759

**Iris Inn *
191 Chinquapin Dr
Waynesboro, VA   22980-5692
540-943-1991**

WEYERS CAVE
Inn at Keezletown Rd *
RR 1 Box 14
Weyers Cave, VA   24486-9703
540-234-0644

WHITE POST
L'Auberge Provencale
PO Box 119
White Post, VA   22663-0119
540-837-1375

WILLIAMSBURG
**Applewood Colonial B & B *
605 Richmond Rd
Williamsburg, VA   23185
757-229-0205**

**Colonial Capital B&B *
501 Richmond Rd
Williamsburg, VA   23185
757-229-0233**

Fox Grape Inn
700 Monumental Ave
Williamsburg, VA   23185-4505
757-229-6914

Castles at Williamsburg
711 Goodwin St
Williamsburg, VA   23185-3910

**Cedaras *
616 Jamestown Rd
Williamsburg, VA 23185
757-229-3591**

Governor's Trace B&B *
303 Capitol Landing Rd
Williamsburg, VA   23185
757-229-7552

Magnolia Manor *
700 Richmond Rd
Williamsburg, VA   23185
757-220-9600

Candelwick B&B*
800 Jamestown Rd
Williamsburg, VA   23185
757-253-8693

Primrose *
706 Richmond Rd
Williamsburg, VA 23185
757-229-6421

Hite's B&B
704 Monumental Ave
Williamsburg, VA 23185-4505
757-229-4814

Holland's Lodge *
601 Richmond Rd
Williamsburg, VA 23185-3539
757-253-6476

Legacy of Williamsburg Tavern
930 Jamestown Rd
Williamsburg, VA 23185-3917
757-220-0524

Liberty Rose B&B
1022 Jamestown Rd
Williamsburg, VA 23185-3434
757-253-1260

Newport House B&B *
710 S Henry St
Williamsburg, VA 23185-4113
757-229-1775

Williamsburg Sampler B&B *
922 Jamestown Rd
Williamsburg, VA 23185-3917
757-253-0398

War Hill Inn
4560 Longhill Rd
Williamsburg, VA 23188-1533

Lake B&B
303 Capitol Landing Rd
Williamsburg, VA 23185-4314

Indian Springs Bed & Breakfast
330 Indian Springs Rd
Williamsburg, VA 23185-
757-220-0726

WOODSTOCK
Azalea House B&B *
551 S. Main St
Woodstock, VA 22664
540-459-3900

Country Fare
402 N. Main St
Woodstock, VA 22664
540-459-4828

Inn at Narrow Passage *
PO Box 608
Woodstock, VA 22664-0608
540-849-8000

Candlewick Inn
127 N Church St
Woodstock, VA 22664-1712
540-459-8008

Innkeepers
RR 1 Box 217A
Woodstock, VA 22664-9740

River'd Inn
Rt 1, Box 217-A1
Woodstock, VA 22664
540-459-5369

WOOLWINE
Mountain Rose B&B *
RR 1 Box 280
Woolwine, VA 24185
540-930-1057

RESERVATION SERVICE ORGANIZATIONS

Each of these RSOs covers a geographic area serving about 50-200 inspected properties on their roster.

Amanda's Bed & Breakfast
1428 Park Avenue
Baltimore, Md 21217
410-225-0001

B & B Tidewater Virginia
P.O. Box 3343
Norfolk, VA 23514
757-627-1983
757-627-9409

Benson House of Richmond
2036 Monument Avenue
Richmond, VA 23220
804-648-7560
804-353-6900

Blue Ridge B & B
Rock & Rills Farm
Rt 2, Box 3895
Berryville, VA 22611
540-955-1246

Guesthouses B & B
P.O. Box 5737
Charlottesville, VA 22905
804-979-7264

Lamplighters Service
RR 7, Box 96G
Lynchburg, VA 24503-9612

Princely Bed & Breakfast
819 Prince Street
Alexandria, VA 22314
703-683-2159

Rockbridge Reservations
Sleep Hollow
P.O. Box 76
Brownsburg, VA 24415
703-348-5698

The Travel Tree
P.O. Box 838
Williamsburg, VA 23185
757-253-1571

Virginia Tourism Office
1629 K Street N.W.
Washington, D.C. 20006
800-934-9184
202-659-5523

TOURIST PROMOTION AGENCIES

ABINGDON
Town of Abingdon
208 W. Main St.
Abingdon, VA 24210
540-676-2282

ALEXANDRIA
Convention & Visitors Bureau
221 King St.
Alexandria, VA 22314
703-838-4200

ALLEGHANY HIGHLANDS
Chamber of Commerce
241 West Main St.
Covington, VA 24426
540-962-2178

ARLINGTON
Convention & Vistors Bureau
2100 Clarendon Boulevard
Suite 608
Arlington, VA 22201
703-358-3520

ASHLAND/HANOVER
Chamber of Commerce
112 N. Railroad Ave.
Ashland, VA 23005
804-798-1722

BEDFORD
Chamber of Commerce
305 East Main St.
Bedford, VA 24523
540-586-9401

BLACKSBURG
Chamber of Commerce
141 Jackson Street
Blacksburg, VA 24060

BLUE RIDGE PARKWAY
P.O. Box 453
Asheville, NC 28802
704-627-3419

BRISTOL
Visitor & Convention Council
P.O. Box 519
Bristol, VA 24203
540-968-4399

CHARLES CITY
County Tourism Board
501 Shirley Plantation Rd.
Charles City, VA 23030
804-829-5121

CHARLOTTESVILLE
Convention & Visitors Bureau
P.O. Box 161
Charlottesville, VA 22902
804-293-6789

CHINCOTEAGUE
Chamber of Commerce
P.O. Box 258
Chincoteague, VA 23336
804-336-6161

CULPEPER
Chamber of Commerce
133 W. Davis St.
Culpeper, VA 22701
540-825-1449

DANVILLE
Chamber of Commerce
P.O. Box 1538
Danville, VA 24543
804-793-5422

EASTERN SHORE
Virginia Tourism Commission
P.O. Drawer R
Melfa, VA 23410
804-787-2460

FAIRFAX COUNTY
Tourism & Convention Bureau
8300 Boone Blvd.
Suite 450
Vienna, VA 22182
703-790-3329

FAUQUIER COUNTY
Chamber of Commerce
P.O. Box 127
Warrenton, VA 22186
540-347-4414

FRANKLIN COUNTY
Chamber of Commerce
P.O. Box 158
Rocky Mount, VA 24151
540-483-9542

FREDERICKSBURG
Department of Tourism
706 Caroline St.
Fredericksburg, VA 22401
540-373-1776

FRONT ROYAL
Chamber of Commerce &
Vistor Center
P.O. Box 568
Front Royal, VA 22630
800-338-2576

GILES COUNTY
Chamber of Commerce
604 Wenonah Ave.
Pearisburg, VA 24134
540-921-5000

HAMPTON
Dept. of Conventions & Tourism
2 Eaton St., Suite 106
Hampton, VA 23669
804-722-1222

HARRISONBURG
Convention & Tourism Bureau
P.O. Box 1
Harrisonburg, VA 22801
540-434-2319

HOPEWELL
Visitors Center
201 D Randolph Sq.
Hopewell, VA 23860
804-541-2206

ISLE OF WIGHT COUNTY
Tourism Bureau
P.O. box 37
Isle of Wight, VA 23430
757-357-5182

KING GEORGE COUNTY
Gateway Travel Center
P.O. Box 71
King George, VA 22485
540-663-3205

LEXINGTON
Visitors Bureau
102 E. Washington St.
Lexington, VA 24450
540-463-3777

LOUDOUN COUNTY
Conference & Visitors Bureau
108-D South St. S.E.
Leesburg, VA 22705
703-777-0518

LYNCHBURG
Dept. of Economic Dev.
P.O. Box 60
Lynchburg, VA 24505
804-847-1654

NEW RIVER VALLEY
Visitors Center
Rt. 1, Box 123-F
Dublin VA 24084
540-674-1100, ext. 154

NEWPORT NEWS
Tourist Info. Center
13560 Jefferson Ave.
Newport News, VA 23603
804-886-7777

NORFOLK
Convention & Visitors Bureau
236 E. Plume St.
Norfolk, VA 23510
757-441-5266

NORTHERN NECK
Travel Council
P.O. Box 312
Reedville, Va 22539
804-453-3915

ORANGE COUNTY
Visitors Bureau
154 Madison Rd.
Orange, Va 22960
540-672-1653

PAGE COUNTY
Chamber of Commerce
46 East Main St.
Luray, VA 22835
540-743-3915

PETERSBURG
Dept. of Tourism
15 West Bank St.
Petersburg, VA 23803
804-733-2402

PORTSMOUTH
Department of Tourism
801 Crawford St.
Portsmouth, VA 23704
757-393-8481

PRINCE WILLIAM
Conference & Visitors Bureau
4349 Ridgewood Ctr. Dr.
Prince William, VA 22192
703-792-6680

RICHMOND
Convention & Visitors Bureau
300 E. Main St.
Suite 100
Richmond, VA 23219
804-782-2777

ROANOKE VALLEY
Convention & Visitors Bureau
114 Market St.
Roanoke, VA 24011
540-342-6025

SHENANDOAH COUNTY
P.O. Box 452
Woodstock, VA 22664
540-459-5522

SMITH MOUNTAIN LAKE
Lake Partnership
2 Bridgewater Plaza
Moneta, VA 24121
540-721-1203

SOUTH HILL
Chamber of Commerce
201 S. Mecklenburg Ave
South Hill, VA 23970
804-447-4547

SPOTSYLVANIA
Visitors Center
4704 Southpoint Parkway
Fredericksburg, VA 22407
540-891-8687

STAUNTON
Tourism Coordinator
P.O. Box 58
Staunton, VA 24401
540-332-3865

VIRGINIA BEACH
Convention & Visitors Dev.
2101 Parks Ave.
Suite 500
Virginia Beach, VA 23451
757-437-4700

WAYNESBORO
Chamber of Commerce
301 West Main St.
Waynesboro, VA 22980
540-949-8203

WILLIAMSBURG
Convention & Visitors Bureau
201 Penniman Rd.
Williamsburg, VA 23187
757-253-0192

WINCHESTER
Visitor Center
1360 Pleasant Valley Rd.
Winchester, VA 22601
540-662-4118

WISE COUNTY
Chamber of Commerce
903 Virginia Ave.
Norton, VA 24273
540-679-0961

WYTHEVILLE
Dir. of Public Info.
P.O. Box 533
Wytheville, VA 24382
540-228-3111